Praise for
The Haves and the Have-Nots

"Where do *you* rank in the all-time world distribution of income? How about Jane Austen's Mr. Darcy? Or Anna Karenina? Was Octavian Augustus richer than Bill Gates? Why might China fall apart, like the USSR and Yugoslavia? Why should we care about differences in income and wealth? In this book of many delights, Branko Milanovic, who has spent twenty-five years studying global inequality, provides us with a veritable *Arabian Nights* of stories about inequality, drawing from history, literature, and everywhere in the world. A pleasure to read, and an eye-opener for haves and for have-nots alike."

—ANGUS DEATON,
Professor of Economics and International Affairs,
Princeton University, 2009 President of the American
Economic Association, author of *The Analysis of Household
Surveys: A Microeconometric Approach to Development Policy*

"Learn about the serious subject of economic inequality while you have plenty of fun traveling around the globe and far back in time! Through fascinating stories and wonderful illustrations, Branko Milanovic explains income and wealth inequality—their concepts, measurement, evolution, and role in human life—without compromising precision or balance. This is a delightful book, as commendable for vacations as for the classroom."

—THOMAS POGGE,
Professor of Philosophy and International Affairs,
Yale University, author of *World Poverty and Human Rights:
Cosmopolitan Responsibilities and Reforms*

THE HAVES

and the

HAVE-NOTS

A Brief and Idiosyncratic History
of Global Inequality

BRANKO MILANOVIC

BASIC BOOKS
A Member of the Perseus Books Group
New York

Published by Basic Books,
A Member of the Perseus Books Group

Books published by Basic Books are available at special
discounts for bulk purchases in the United States by
corporations, institutions, and other organizations. For more
information, please contact the Special Markets Department at
the Perseus Books Group, 2300 Chestnut Street, Suite 200,
Philadelphia, PA 19103, or call (800) 810-4145, ext. 5000,
or e-mail special.markets@perseusbooks.com.

Designed by Brent Wilcox

Library of Congress Cataloging-in-Publication Data
Milanovic, Branko.
    The haves and the have-nots : a brief and idiosyncratic
history of global inequality / Branko Milanovic.
        p.   cm.
    Includes bibliographical references and index.
    ISBN 978-0-465-01974-8 (alk. paper)
    1. Income distribution—History.   2. Wealth—
History.   3. Poverty—History.   I. Title.
    HC79.I5M547 2010
    339.2—dc22
                                                2010029295

10 9 8 7 6 5 4 3 2 1

For N. and G.

"To determine the laws which regulate this
distribution [into wages, profits and rent],
is the principal problem in Political Economy."

David Ricardo, *Principles of*
Political Economy **(1817)**

"Of the tendencies that are harmful to sound
economics, the most seductive, and . . . the most
poisonous, is to focus on questions of distribution."

Robert E. Lucas, "The Industrial Revolution:
Past and Future" (2004)

Contents

Contents

CHAPTER 3
Essay III: Unequal World
Inequality Among Citizens in the World 149

Preface

This book is about income and wealth inequality in history and today. Inequality appeared as soon as human society was born, because distinctions of power and wealth accompany all human societies.[1] Inequality is by definition social, since it is a relational phenomenon (I can be unequal only if there is somebody else). Inequality can thus exist only when there is a society. A Robinson Crusoe cannot have a concept of equality, but Robinson Crusoe and his Man Friday do. Moreover, inequality makes even more sense when society is not a mechanical accumulation of individuals but a group of people who share certain characteristics such as common government, language, religion, or historical memories.

The objective of the stories around which this book is organized is to show, in an unusual and entertaining way, how inequality of income and wealth is present in many facets of our daily lives, in the stories we read or the discussions we have around our kitchen tables or in our schools or offices, and how inequality appears when we look at certain well-known phenomena from a different angle. The objective is to unveil the importance that differences in income and wealth, affluence and poverty, play in our ordinary lives as well as the importance that they have had historically.

The book is organized around three types of inequalities. In the first part, I deal with inequality among individuals within a single community—typically, a nation. This is the type of inequality that most of us will easily recognize because it is the type of inequality that we are likely to think of first when we hear the word *inequality*. In the second part, I deal with inequality in income among countries or nations—which is also intuitively close to most of us because it is the sort of thing we notice when we travel, or when we watch the international news. In some countries most people appear poor to us, while in others most people seem very affluent. These "between-country" inequalities find their expression also in migration when workers from poor countries move to the rich world in order to earn more and enjoy a higher standard of living. In the third part, I move to the topic whose relevance and importance are of much more recent vintage: global inequality, or inequality among all citizens of the world. This inequality is the sum of the previous two inequalities: that of individuals within nations and that among nations. But it is a new topic because only with globalization have we become used to contrasting and comparing our own fortunes with the fortunes of individual people around the globe. Yet it is probably a type of inequality whose importance will, as the process of globalization unfolds, increase the most.

I've illustrated each type of inequality with short stories (vignettes), some of which take us all the way back to Roman times, while others could be almost taken from the daily newspapers—Barack Obama's family, the global middle class, or Maghrebi migrants to Europe. Each of the vignettes can be read separately, and they do not need to be read in order. In some cases, however, the vignettes are linked by their topic, and reading them in succession might be more appealing. Yet they are all stand-alone pieces.

Each part is introduced by an essay on what economists have to say about that particular type of inequality. The essays, while written to be accessible to all interested readers, are probably a little bit more demanding in terms of attention than the vignettes. They are supposed to provide the reader with a better technical grasp of the issues that are discussed in the vignettes. For those readers who may be perhaps keen to pursue the issues in the book further, the essays offer an introduction to the literature. At the end of the book, in "Further Readings," I also include a list of selected publications, arranged by essay and vignette, that readers may consult if they would like to know more. The books and articles listed are my own choices of what I consider the most interesting and relevant publications for a given topic.

On a personal note, this book was not only a pleasure to write but also a very easy undertaking. After working for more than a quarter of a century on the issue of inequality, I have amassed a huge amount of data, information, and interesting stories, and have it literally at my fingertips. I thought that they would be fun to share with the readers. When I sat down to write the book, I did not have to think much about what to include or how to shape it. It was just a question of writing down all the things on which I had thought quite a lot already, and for quite some time, and for which I had ready-made data. Perhaps most important from a personal perspective, this book has given me the opportunity to combine my two passions: a passion for numbers and distributions and a passion for history.

I had three objectives, and, of course, like every author, I do not know if I was able to achieve any of them. First, I would like for the reader to pass some pleasant time reading the stories and hope that he or she will be able to combine the pleasure of easy reading with the learning of new facts or of a fresh way of looking at things. Second, I thought it important to bring to the attention of the public the issues of inequality in wealth and income that, for many reasons (some "objective" and some perhaps dictated by the interests of the rich), have tended to be swept under the carpet so that they do not "disturb" the public too much. Third, bringing the issues of wealth and poverty to the center of a social debate, particularly at a time of crisis, should stimulate some old-fashioned social activism. In other words, people have the right to start asking questions about the justification of certain incomes and the huge gaps that exist between the rich and poor in most countries, including the United States, and between the rich and poor countries in the world. These are the issues that some dominant segments of public opinion makers have tended to discard, all too easily, I believe, by arguing that all or almost all inequalities are market determined and as such should not be the object of discussion. But neither are many of them market determined, but rather determined by relative political power (as the examples—all too numerous—of the global financial crisis show), nor can the questioning be taken out of the social arena by evoking "the market." The market economy is a social construct, created, or rather discovered, to serve people, and thus raising questions about the way it functions is fully legitimate in every democratic society.

I have to end the Preface with a technical note. The reader will discover as he or she goes through the book that it contains the results of a lot of calculations. All the calculations whose sources are not explicitly given in the footnotes are my own unpublished calculations, based on various data sources, mostly those from the World Bank and World Income Distribution (WYD) databases, which contain a lot of macro data and several hundred household surveys from most countries in the world. I thought that it would be unduly tedious to list such sources for each and every number that I have produced. If the reader is particularly interested in a given fact or calculation, I would be delighted to supply the exact source (since the sources are all on my laptop anyway!). He or she can write to my e-mail address (bmilanovic@worldbank.org or branko_mi@yahoo.com). For all other data, which were taken from other authors and their publications, the sources are clearly indicated in the text.

It is a pleasure to acknowledge the assistance and support that I have received from many individuals. Because this book is in some ways the result of more than twenty years of work on this topic, the list of people whom I should acknowledge would have to be huge and include practically everybody whom I have met and from whom I have learned something. I, obviously, cannot do that. So I have to limit it only to the people who were very directly involved in the production of this volume. They are acknowledged at the beginning of each vignette or essay on which I have sought their advice, comments, and suggestions. In addition to them, I am grateful to Tim Sullivan and Melissa Veronesi, my editors, who have shaped the organization of the book; Annette Wenda, who has carefully gone through every sentence; Michele Alacevich and Valentina Kalk, on whose substantive and aesthetic advice I have much depended; Gouthami Padam, who has worked with me for more than seven years; Shaohua Chen, whose assistance on Chinese household surveys was invaluable; Leif Wenar, to whose advice regarding issues of political philosophy and in particular the interpretation of John

Rawls's works I have frequently turned and who has given me excellent comments on several parts of the manuscript; and Slaheddine Khenissi, for his vast knowledge of the Arab and Muslim worlds. Of course, the responsibility for the opinions expressed in this book is solely my own.

CHAPTER 1

ESSAY I

Unequal People

Inequality Among Individuals Within a Nation

Until about the turn of the twentieth century, income in-equality among individuals was subsumed under the topic of the functional distribution of national income—that is, how total income was split between large social classes (workers and capitalists).[1] It was considered by many to be the key topic in political economy. Society, under early capitalism of the nineteenth century, seemed normally to divide into several quite distinct social classes: workers, who were selling labor and earning wages, and were relatively poor; capitalists, who owned capital and were earning profits, and were relatively rich; and landlords, who owned land and received rents, and were also rich. The distribution of income among these three classes was considered of crucial importance for determining the future of a society. English economist David Ricardo, one of the founders of the discipline of political economy, believed that the share of landlords would increase as greater population required more food, which would bring ever less fertile land into cultivation and raise rents. Prices of "wage goods" (food) and landlord's rents would skyrocket. He saw the eventual outcome as a stationary state where low profits, squeezed between the rising prices of food and rents, would provide little incentive to save and invest.[2] Karl Marx saw greater mechanization, expressed in an increasing value of capital per worker, leading to lower returns to capital and over the long run to a tendency of the profit rate to diminish, eventually tending toward zero and choking off investment.

This way of looking at income distribution through the prism of social classes did not change much with the key turning point in the history of economics, the replacement of classical "political economy" by the "marginalist revolution" that started around 1870 and focused on individual optimization rather than on broad economic evolution of social classes, nor did it change later with the synthesis of the two strands (classical and marginalist) under the title of "neoclassical Marshallian economics" (from the Cambridge economist Alfred Marshall) and its establishment in the mainstream position. It was only in the early 1900s that the distribution of income among individuals (not among classes) attracted the attention of Vilfredo Pareto, a Franco-Italian economist who taught at the University of Lausanne in Switzerland. (His contribution is highlighted in Vignette 1.10.)

It was around the same time that the data on personal income distribution became available for the first time. This went hand in hand with economic development (countries becoming richer) and a broader fiscal role of the state. The early statistical information about income distribution emerged because of nation-states' need to collect direct taxes in a "fairer" way—that is, according to income—and to increase total tax intake, to spend it for public education, workers' invalidity, and, above all, war. The ideological change that saw all individuals as equal before the law, and thus the rich due to contribute more in accordance with their greater wealth and income, was important, too. Taxes had to be more tightly linked to income, and this required better information on incomes and their distribution among households. It is thus not surprising that the data used by Pareto to study income distribution among persons all came from the European late-nineteenth-century fiscal sources. At that point, our topic had been born.

Economists and social scientists are concerned with inequality in three ways. The first type of question they ask is: What determines inequality among individuals within a single nation? Are there certain regularities that make inequality behave in a particular way as societies develop? Does inequality increase as the economy expands—that is, is it pro- or anticyclical? In these types of questions, inequality is something that ought to be explained. It is a dependent variable. In the second type of question, inequality enters as a variable that explains other economic phenomena. Is high or low inequality good for economic growth, for better governance, for attracting foreign investments, for spreading education among the population, and so on? In these instances, we look at inequality in a purely instrumental sense: We are interested in whether it furthers or hampers some particular desirable economic outcome. The third way inequality enters within the social scientists' purview is when they address ethical issues linked with it. In these cases, they are concerned with the justice of social arrangements that exhibit different amounts of inequality. Is increasing inequality acceptable only if it raises the absolute incomes of the poor? Should inequality due to one's better family circumstances be treated differently than inequality due to superior work and effort?

How does inequality change with the income level of a society? Pareto, basing his work on a limited sample of the late-nineteenth-century tax data from European countries and cities, believed in an "iron law of inter-personal inequality," such that differences in social arrangements (whether a society is feudalist, capitalist, or socialist) leave distribution more or less unchanged. The elites could be different; they may control society differently, but the distribution of income—and therefore the level of inequality—will not be much affected. Today, this is popularly called the "80/20 law," expressing the finding that in some phenomena, we observe a regularity such that 20 percent of people are responsible for 80 percent of outcomes and the reverse (the other 80 percent of people generate only 20 percent of outcomes). It has been argued that the 80/20 law is found in quality control (80 percent of problems are due to 20 percent of products) and marketing and business applications, and we shall see something similar to hold even for global income distribution (see Essay III). As for income distribution within nations, Pareto failed to define a theory of change in it, although "failure" is not a wholly appropriate term simply because Pareto thought, and believed to have empirically proved, that income distribution must be more or less fixed and thus that there were no laws of its "change" with development. There was, Pareto argued, only a "law of its fixity."

It wasn't until 1955 that Simon Kuznets, a Russian-American economist and statistician, proposed the first real theory of what propels change in income distribution. (He is profiled, together with Pareto, in Vignette 1.10.) He argued—having had access to not many more data points than Pareto (although the data were of a different kind, household, not fiscal, surveys)—that inequality among people is *not* the same regardless of the type of society but varies predictably as society develops. Inequality in very poor societies must be low because the income of the vast majority of the population is just around subsistence, and there is little economic distinction among people. Then, as an economy develops and people move from agriculture into industry, Kuznets posited, a gap emerges in average earnings between industrial workers (richer) and farmers (poorer). The industrial sector also sees more differentiation in incomes between individual workers than is the case among farmers simply because tasks required by modern industry are more diversified. Therefore, income inequality increases both because of the growing gap in average earnings between industry and agriculture and because of rising inequality among industrial workers. Finally, in even more advanced societies, the state begins to play a redistributive role (see Vignette 1.7), education becomes more widespread, and inequality goes down (see Vignettes 1.1 and 1.2). Thus was formulated the famous "Kuznets' hypothesis" of an inverted U curve charted by income inequality in the course of economic development: Inequality must first increase before it goes down.

The idea, however, was not entirely novel. It was expressed some 120 years earlier by French social scientist and politician Alexis de Tocqueville and is worth quoting in full:

> If one looks closely at what has happened to the world since the beginning of society, it is easy to see that equality is prevalent only at the historical poles of civilization. Savages

are equal because they are equally weak and ignorant. Very civilized men can all become equal because they all have at their disposal similar means of attaining comfort and happiness. Between these two extremes is found inequality of condition, wealth, knowledge—the power of the few, the poverty, ignorance, and weakness of all the rest. (*Memoir on Pauperism* [1835]).

But, of course, Tocqueville, not being an economist like Kuznets, did not say anything beyond this, in particular about the mechanism whereby this inverted U shape would be brought into existence.

Kuznets' hypothesis has been empirically tested and retested by economists ever since it was first published in 1955. The ever-greater availability of national household surveys of income and consumption, the key source of information on income distribution, has greatly advanced the empirical exploration of Kuznets' hypothesis. In principle, the hypothesis should work best when we study the evolution of inequality in a single country, as the country undergoes radical transformation from agricultural to industrial and eventually to service-oriented economy. But in that context, its performance has been mixed: Some countries (and over some time periods) exhibited an inverted U pattern, while others did not.

The dissatisfaction with the performance and predictive capacity of Kuznets' hypothesis led to the addition of new elements that could better explain the behavior of income inequality. The revisions are known as the "augmented" Kuznets' hypothesis. Factors such as the "financial depth" of an economy, extent of government spending or state-sector employment, openness of the economy, and so forth now appear alongside income level as possible additional variables that explain the movement of inequality. Many economists argued that these additional elements could improve our understanding of the movement of inequality. For instance, the rationale was that a more efficient and broader financial sector would allow poor individuals to borrow to finance their own educations, and this would reduce inequality as the doors of educational advancement are thrown open to all and not reserved only for the rich. Government spending (as a share of gross domestic product, or GDP) or government employment (as a share of the total labor force) are supposed to have a dampening effect on inequality, first because it helps the poor, and second because it limits wage inequality. Greater openness to trade should, in poor countries, reduce inequality as it increases the demand for low-skill intensive products (say, textiles) in which these countries specialize; this would tend to raise the wages of unskilled workers compared to the wages of skilled workers or the profits of capitalists. In rich countries, openness to trade should produce the opposite effects since rich countries tend to export high-tech products. Their production requires highly skilled workers (say, computer scientists or engineers), so the earnings of college graduates increase relative to those with only a primary or secondary education. Thus, inequality goes up. Economists would test a typical Kuznets' hypothesis today by including all of these factors, and possibly quite a few others, in addition to income, often in an ad hoc fashion (e.g., adding age composition of the population or distribution of landownership). The results are better than when we use income level alone, but hardly spectacular.

More recently, French economist Thomas Piketty has produced a series of empirical studies, conducted jointly with a
number of other economists (Emmanuel Saez, Anthony Atkinson, Abhijit Banerjee) and covering about a dozen countries,
which have undermined both the Kuznets' and the augmented
Kuznets' hypotheses. Piketty shows that after a long downward
swing, inequality in Western nations has decisively increased in
the past quarter of a century. Although these facts were well
known before, Piketty has provided a "political" explanation, explaining them by governments' decisions to increase or decrease
direct taxation of current income and inherited wealth as well as
by the effects of wars (i.e., destruction of physical capital and reduced income of capitalists). This is arguably a political theory
of income distribution where social attitudes (of what is just or
unjust) and economic interests, reflected through voting and
stances of political parties, as well as the war needs of economies,
determine the path that inequality charts over time.

Piketty's studies, in order to explain what moves inequality
over a long time period (the entire twentieth century), resorted
to an old and rather discarded source of data: fiscal statistics.
The reason fiscal statistics, first used by Pareto, have been replaced by household surveys is that fiscal data cover only a
portion—the higher end—of income distribution since in most
countries direct taxes are not paid by the poor. Household surveys, on the contrary, include everyone. The problem with the
use of fiscal data is that conclusions drawn from them are valid
only if the following two assumptions hold: (1) Taxable incomes
are reasonable approximations of actual incomes of households
(and the highest taxpayers are also the richest people), and (2) the
evolution of overall inequality can be well approximated by the

change in the share of the top income groups (say, the top 1 percent of taxpayers whom we believe to be also the richest 1 percent of households). Neither assumption is fully defensible. Taxable income used by Piketty and coauthors is called *market* (or *pre-fisc*) income, which excludes both taxes paid and government transfers.[3] However, we are normally interested in what happens to inequality of *disposable* income, that is, income that belongs to households and individuals *after* they have paid taxes and received government transfers. Thus, if either taxes or transfers change, market and disposable income inequality can move in different directions. The problem with the second assumption is that inequality statistics should, in principle, include incomes of all people, not focus only on the rich. It could, for example, happen that the income share of the top increases while the income share of the poor goes up as well and both do so at the expense of the middle-class share. We may then not be able to say that the overall inequality went up, as we would tend to conclude solely from the rising income share of the top. Since Piketty-type studies depend on this particular assumption (which we know does not hold in all places and times), the interpretation of the results becomes problematic. Of course, if we had income or consumption surveys of the population for the periods sufficiently far in the past, the problem would be solved. We would not need to resort to the much less precise and fragmentary fiscal data. Unfortunately (as we shall see below), such surveys are available in rich countries generally only for the period after World War II and for many developing countries only for the past twenty or thirty years.

This is the situation of inequality studies today. It would be unfair or even impossible to summarize which of these different points of view has won the debate. Probably none. But it does lead to the question beyond simply measuring inequality or understanding how it evolves, and gets to the heart of whether inequality is necessary for an economy to grow and, if so, how high it should be.

How does inequality affect economic efficiency? We care about inequality, or perhaps we care mostly about inequality, because we believe that it affects some important economic phenomena—notably, economic growth: Do more unequal countries grow faster or slower? Historically, the pendulum has swung from a rather unambiguous answer that inequality is good for growth to a much more nuanced view that favors the opposite conclusion.

Why has this been the case? To understand it, look at inequality, as far as economic efficiency is concerned, as cholesterol: There is "good" and "bad" inequality, just as there is good and bad cholesterol.[4] "Good" inequality is needed to create incentives for people to study, work hard, or start risky entrepreneurial projects. None of that can be done without providing some inequality in returns (for the effects of "unreasonable" leveling of incomes, see Vignette 1.5 on inequality under socialism). But "bad" inequality starts at a point—one not easy to define—where, rather than providing the motivation to excel, inequality provides the means to preserve acquired positions. This happens when inequality in wealth or income is used to forestall an economically positive political change for the society (e.g., agrarian reform or abolition of slavery), or to allow only the rich to get education, or to ensure that the rich keep the best jobs. All of this undercuts economic efficiency. If one's ability to get a good education strongly depends on one's parents' wealth, this is equivalent to depriving society of the skills and knowledge of a large segment of its members (the poor). Discrimination according to inherited income is not, in that sense, different from any other discrimination, such as gender or race. In all cases, society decides that the skills of a certain group of people will not be used. Economically, such societies are unlikely to be successful. Depending on which kind of inequality—"positive," needed for incentives, or "negative," ensuring monopoly of the rich—is dominant in a given country and time, inequality may be regarded as either beneficial or harmful.

The benevolent view of economic inequality—that it provides incentives for individuals to excel—dominated when economists believed that only the very rich save and that without them, there would be no investments and no wealth creation. Workers (or the poor) were thought apt to spend everything they earned. If everybody then had the same (relatively) low income, there would be no saving, no investment, and no economic growth. The rich per se were not important, but it was important to have them around so that they would save, augment capital, and provide the wherewithal for feeding the engine of economic growth. The rich were supposed to be receptacles for the individualization of savings. They would spend and enjoy themselves no more than the others. All the excess would be simply saved and invested. Asceticism, as Max Weber wrote, was the key ingredient of such a "spirit of capitalism": "The *summum bonum* of this ethic, the earning of more and more money, combined with the strict avoidance of all spontaneous enjoyment of life, is above all completely devoid of any . . . hedonistic admixture. It is thought of so purely as an end in itself, that from the point of view of happiness of, or utility to, the single individual, it appears entirely . . . irrational."[5]

It is in the passage written in 1920 by John Maynard Keynes, famous English economist and founder of modern macroeconomics, that this slightly rose-tinted view of the justification of inequality of incomes under the condition that high incomes be used for investment finds perhaps its best expression:

> Society [of pre-1914 Europe] was so framed as to throw a great part of the increased income into the control of the class least likely to consume it. The new rich of the nineteenth century were not brought up to large expenditures, and preferred the power which investment gave them to the pleasures of immediate consumption. In fact, it was precisely the *inequality* of the distribution of wealth which made possible those vast accumulations of fixed wealth and of capital improvements which distinguished that age from all others. Herein lay, in fact, the main justification of the Capitalist System. If the rich had spent their new wealth on their own enjoyments, the world would long ago have found such a régime intolerable. But like bees they saved and accumulated, not less to the advantage of the whole community because they themselves held narrower ends in prospect.[6]

This was the view of capitalists as "saving machines" and entrepreneurs.

But the world was also full of another type of capitalist rentiers who would do very little but sit back, relax, and let money "do the work" for them. For a literary description of rentiers we can go to Stefan Zweig's beautiful book about the "world of yesterday," pre–World War I Europe, a world where the most cherished compliment (as Zweig writes) was "solid," the highest value bourgeois respectability, and reasonableness and progress seemed destined to go on forever. For the rich, the living was easy:

> Thanks to the constant accumulation of profits, in an era of increasing prosperity in which the State never thought of nibbling off more than a few percent of income of even the richest, and in which . . . State and industrial bonds bore high rates of interest, to grow richer was nothing more than a passive activity for the wealthy.[7]

From this perspective, the rich looked less indispensable as "receptacles" for savings and as possible investors; they appeared much more like parasites living well while clipping coupons and doing little else. Yet the view of inequality as harmful, which began to dominate in the past couple of decades, did not develop from that ethical perspective. Curiously, it shares the same starting point with the view of inequality as a benevolent force— namely, that there should be people who are willing to invest—yet it reaches very different conclusions. Here's how the argument flows[8]: People (rich, middle class, and poor) vote for how high they want their taxes to be, taking into account that the advantages from government spending (funded from taxes) accrue mostly to the poor. Very unequal societies will tend to vote for high taxation simply because there are a lot of people who benefit from government transfers, pay nothing or little in taxes, and would always outvote the few rich (see Vignette 1.7). Now, such high taxation reduces the incentives to invest and to work hard, and this lowers the rate of economic growth. The mechanism is similar to the nineteenth-century fear that people without property, if given half a chance to vote, would expropriate the wealthy. Here the same thing happens except that the expropriation is a bit gentler: It operates not through outright nationalization but through taxation.[9]

In both cases—the benign and the malevolent views of economic inequality—the important thing is to have people who are willing to invest. But in the first case, rich investors require high inequality. In the second case, the introduction of political democracy is the monkey wrench that makes high inequality politically unsustainable. Even if the rich could somehow promise the poor that they would not consume but invest surplus income, and that the rich are thus indispensable for economic growth, there is no way that this promise could be enforced. It will not be credible, either. Consequently, the capitalist system must generate on its own a pre-tax income distribution that is sustainable and will not encourage people to choose extortionary tax rates. For this to happen, assets among people need to be distributed relatively evenly. We cannot, over the short or medium term, affect the distribution of financial assets much, but we can affect the distribution of education (what economists call "human capital")—hence the emphasis on better access to education for everybody. This is not only because education may be thought desirable in itself, not even because higher education may be directly helpful for economic growth, but also because wider distribution of that asset would equalize distribution of pre-tax income and make even those relatively poor think twice before deciding to vote for high taxes.

Does a change in economic development also produce a change in our view of the usefulness of inequality? Quite likely.[10] In the early stages of development, physical capital is scarce. It is then important to have rich people who are ready not to consume their entire income but to invest it so that more machines and roads can be built. As the economy develops, physical capital becomes less scarce, and relative to it, human capital (education) becomes more valuable. It is then crucial to spread education. But if the spread of education is constrained because talented children of the poor cannot pay for education, the growth rate will sputter. Thus, even without the introduction of universal voting rights and democracy, we reach a similar conclusion: For growth to be fast, at higher stages of economic development, education must be widespread, and widespread education is tantamount to less inequality.

The empirical evidence of the effect of inequality on economic growth is mixed. Perhaps this is inevitable because in some places and times, inequality may hamper economic growth (through its monopoly element) and in others help it (through its incentive element). Suffice it to say that our view regarding the positive versus negative effects of inequality on economic efficiency will always depend on how much weight we put on one or the other element in the essential dilemma: social monopoly versus incentives. In those cases where we believe that the monopoly of power and wealth exercised by the rich threatens social stability, and with it economic development and even the viability of a state, we would, as Plato did 2,400 years ago, see income or wealth inequality as a social evil to be combated. Asked whether his laying down of austerity as a desirable feature of his ideal state would not expose it to the danger of conquest from richer neighbors, Socrates (in Plato's words) replies:

"But what should we call the others [communities that are not an ideal state]?," he asked.[11]

"We ought to find a grander name for them," [Socrates] replied. "Each of them is, as the proverb says, not so much a single state as a collection of states. For it always contains at least two states, the rich and the poor, at enmity with each other. . . . Treat them as plurality, offer to hand over the property . . . of one section [of population] to another, and you will have allies in plenty and very few enemies."[12]

But in those cases where we think that the leveling of incomes—the absence both of the carrot of success and of the stick of failure—has gone so far that people will not try harder unless allowed to keep the fruits of their labor or investment more fully, we should, as odd as it may seem, opt out and call forth greater inequality.

Inequality and economic justice. Income inequality is also an important topic because it straddles two areas that are often at the center of people's interests but not always or easily reconciled: economic efficiency and economic justice. Economic efficiency deals with the maximization of total output or rate of economic progress of a society. Economic justice deals with the acceptance and sustainability of a given social arrangement. Economic inequality plays an obvious role there, too. Inequality based on one's inheritance, race, or gender may be regarded as unjust even when not detrimental to economic development, that is, above its purely instrumental value. If most people, or an influential minority, regard a given social order as unjust, sustainability of that type of arrangement will be questioned.

Economists tend to use, when assessing the desirability of different social arrangements, the "social welfare function," a construct that in principle includes the welfare (utility) of all members of a community. The objective is to compare the welfare of all members in one social arrangement with the welfare of all members in another and find the better one. This is called "welfarism." A crude way to do it is simply to add individual utilities, so that in a society composed of Alan, Bob, and Charlie, the total utility (or welfare) of the society would be equal to the utility of Alan plus the utility of Bob plus the utility of Charlie. The individual utility functions of Alan, Bob, and Charlie are such that each of them gets positive although decreasing utilities from every additional dollar of income. This is a reasonable and empirically confirmed assumption: Think of the fact that the first ice cream on a hot day will give you more pleasure than the second, and surely even more pleasure than the third. The idea goes under the general title of diminishing marginal utility of income. Now, assume in addition that Alan, Bob, and Charlie have the same utility functions. Then the optimal distribution of income would be one of full equality. If we had given a bit more income to Alan than to Bob and Charlie, we can readily see (since they have diminishing and the same marginal utility functions) that the extra income must give less pleasure to the rich Alan than it would give to the poorer Bob and Charlie. Thus, total utility would increase if we were to keep transferring Alan's extra income up to the point where each person would get the same amount.

This was the idea behind one of the key economic contributions to the welfarist approach, English economist Anthony Atkinson's highly influential 1970 article on the measurement of inequality that would also let us rank the desirability of different social arrangements.[13] Atkinson developed a measure whereby a society's inequality is calculated as that relative amount of total income that is "wasted" from the welfare perspective because the same total welfare could be realized by a smaller overall income equally distributed among individuals. This is somewhat ungainfully called "equally distributed equivalent income." Even if the total pie were smaller but the slices were all of equal size, total pleasure from a smallish pie would be the same as total pleasure from a larger, but unequally sliced pie. Say that Cuba and the Dominican Republic generate the same total amount of welfare among their inhabitants, but the overall Dominican income is higher. Thus, the "excess" part of the Dominican income is really wasted from the utility point of view: Dominicans can just "nix" that extra income, work less hard, and redistribute their smaller income much more equally, as the Cubans do. Ultimately, there would be no loss in welfare. How much income is "wasted" is therefore a measure of inequality.

It is easy to see that if some way of adding up the utilities of different individuals existed, it would be rather easy to say which overall state of affairs (Cuban or Dominican) is preferable. The problem, though, is that there is no generally acceptable way to meaningfully combine individual utilities. We may agree that, in general, all individuals will experience diminishing marginal utility as their consumption of whatever good or service increases. But we cannot compare the *levels* of these utilities: A person may be permanently on a higher level of utility than another. In other words, while the shape of utility functions may be similar (decreasing in income), their levels may vary among individuals. To go back to our example, even if Bob told us that he lives in a state of permanent bliss, we cannot be sure that he is really happier than the curmudgeonly Charlie. They may just be using different utility metrics.

Moreover, even if we knew everyone's exact utility and could then theoretically maximize welfare, there would still be an ethical problem because the distribution that would generate the highest sum of welfare would be such that income is allocated mostly to the individuals who have high utility functions, those that are best in converting given income into utility. This is the idea with which English economist Francis Edgeworth in the late-nineteenth-century used to defend inequality: He argued that the richer people with more "refined" tastes deserve higher incomes because they derive more pleasure from (say) better food or wine. Should a society really be so arranged that it transfers most income to those who can best enjoy it? Should optimal income distribution be such that a few Epicureans who cannot imagine living without champagne and caviar be funded by people who live on bread alone?

This became the basis of Amartya Sen's influential critique, known as the "capability approach": If a handicapped person cannot get as much utility from playing a soccer game as a nonhandicapped person, should we give more and more opportunities to the nonhandicapped and fewer and fewer to the handicapped people simply because the latter do not "produce" (for themselves, and thus for society) as much utility? To one's common sense, this is an abhorrent conclusion. Sen argued that we should try instead to equalize the "capabilities" of each to enjoy themselves.[14]

In a nutshell, when it comes to using welfare judgments to rank different social arrangements, we face three options. First, we can treat everybody's utility function as being the same (which we know not to be the case in real life), which leads to the maximization of total welfare at the point where income is divided exactly equally. This is the idea behind Atkinson's "equally distributed equivalent income." Second, we can try to "seek out" individuals who are more "efficient" generators of utility and give them higher incomes. Or, third, we can do the reverse—give higher incomes precisely to those who, as in Sen's capability approach, are more challenged in enjoying pleasure from a given bundle of goods and services. This could easily reduce the total welfare measured by some simple summation of individual utilities, and we would no longer need to ground our judgments in welfarism.[15]

A more sophisticated welfarist approach consists of constructing a social welfare function where the utility of each member is included but there is no summation of utilities, just the depiction of welfare states attained by each individual. In that case we can rank as preferable only the "states of the world" where at least one person is better off and nobody is worse off. Such states of the world satisfy the so-called Pareto criterion: If we move to them, we can be sure that no one would complain. But the problem with such a requirement is that it is not merely ultraconservative. It is much more than that: It can almost never be found in the real world. Try to think of anything that would satisfy the Pareto criterion: Wouldn't better health care be good for most people? Yes, but some would have to pay more for insurance, and they would object. Would not a miraculous decision to stop consuming addictive drugs be good for so many people? Yes, but drug producers and traders (they are as much people as anyone else) would lose, and they would object. Wouldn't you like to pay lower taxes? Yes, but somebody's Social Security check would not be delivered, and he would veto it. And we can go on. However hard we try, we may never find a policy that would satisfy the Pareto criterion. It is in effect a prescription for

immobility, stagnation, doing nothing, and—most important—
keeping power and privilege where they currently are.

Thus, no less than its cruder form, a more sophisticated "welfarism" too is flawed. Both are hobbled by the inability to make
interpersonal comparisons of utility, and the end result is that
they are of extremely limited use for ranking alternative social
arrangements.[16] In effect, it is difficult to ground a theory of justice of social arrangements in utilitarianism or welfarism. The
great dream of Jeremy Bentham and John Stuart Mill, the fa-
thers of utilitarianism, that an "objective" way of comparing different societies had been discovered, is probably dead.

On the ruins of this dream was built the most famous recent
attempt to provide some guidance on how to reconcile economic
inequality and justice: that of John Rawls, an American political
philosopher. Rawls, in enunciating his celebrated "difference
principle" in *A Theory of Justice* published in 1971, argued that
the justification for any departure from equality can be found
only if it is needed to raise the absolute income of the poorest.
In other words, the baseline position is that of complete economic
equality among citizens. Any departure from it needs justification. Rawls's *Theory of Justice* radically departed from utilitarianism. He stated it rather unambiguously:

> A rational man would not accept a basic structure merely be-
> cause it maximized the algebraic sum of advantages irrespective
> of its permanent effects on his own basic rights and interests.
> Thus it seems that the principle of utility is incompatible with
> the conception of social cooperation among equals for mutual
> advantage. It appears to be inconsistent with the idea of reci-
> procity implicit in the notion of a well-ordered society.[17]

Rawls linked inequality and injustice in one brilliant sentence: "Injustice, then, is simply inequalities that are not to the benefit of all" and "in particular to the poor" (as he would add a couple of paragraphs later).[18] Although inequality and injustice thus became inextricably entwined and Rawls held that the application of his "difference principle" would lead to a relatively narrow distribution of income because many arrangements that privilege the rich are not to the *absolute* advantage of the poor, in principle, the difference principle is compatible with a very wide range of inequality outcomes. It may impose rather strict equality if no increase in the income of the rich is needed to advance the incomes of the poor. But it may also allow for a very wide and rising inequality, where additional gains are disproportionately received by the rich, so long as there is some, albeit very modest, increase in the income of the poor.[19]

Measurement of inequality. Economists' infatuation with utilitarianism has affected, although rather indirectly, another area that has to do with economic inequality: its measurement. The measurement of economic inequality started as a simple axiomatic-based task of devising a reasonable rod by which the inequality of an entire distribution could be summarized in one number. The key axioms are easily understandable. For example, if there is a transfer of income from a richer to a poorer individual and nothing else changes,[20] the measure of inequality should go down; if two people swap positions, the measure should not change (this is known as the anonymity principle); if all incomes are multiplied by a constant, the measure should not change; and so forth.[21] As such, measurement was purely a technical issue, no different from the measurement of temperature. However, the dominant welfarist approach preferred to see these measures as expressing some deeper social welfare–based idea. The difficulties of welfarism are apparent if we, for example, consider the just defined, and very reasonable, anonymity principle. To couch that simple technical requirement in welfarism one must accept the utterly unrealistic notion that all individuals share the same utility function. If they do not, then, from the point of view of utility generation, any two individuals cannot be the same: One, a high utility-generation machine, cannot be easily substituted by a more lethargic "utility-challenged" person.

The tension between an axiom-based measurement of inequality and its welfarist interpretation was apparent from the beginning. Italian economist and statistician Corrado Gini, who developed (as we shall see) the most popular measure of inequality, expressed this dilemma as early as 1921:

> The methods of Italian [anti-welfarist] writers . . . are not . . . comparable to Dalton's [an English economist instrumental in arguing for the welfarist approach] . . . inasmuch as their purpose is to estimate, not the inequality of economic welfare, but the inequality of incomes and wealth, independently of all hypotheses as to the functional relations between these quantities and economic welfare or as to the additive character of the economic welfare of individuals.[22]

The welfarist method that seemed for a long time ascendant among economists has recently been in retreat, both because it has failed to produce much in terms of strong and actionable conclusions ("what state of affairs is better") and because its ultimate basis—utilitarianism—is philosophically weak.

One question—and a central one at that—is how we should go about measuring inequality. To measure inequality we need representative and random surveys of households. They provide detailed income information for everyone included in the survey, and since the surveys are supposed to be representative of a broader community (generally, the entire country), their results can be extrapolated to the level of a whole country. We can use tax data, too, but they will always, even in the very advanced countries where most people pay direct taxes, give us only an incomplete (truncated) distribution. They leave out the poor who do not pay taxes. We cannot use censuses because censuses, covering in principle the entire population of a country, are too big to go very deeply: They collect only the essential information like the data on age, ethnicity, sex, place of residence, and so on, but nothing on income or consumption.

The problem with surveys, though, is that, for most developed countries, the first available surveys start only after World War II. There are some earlier and incomplete surveys from nineteenth-century England and the early-twentieth-century United States and Soviet Russia, but we can hardly speak of anything serious and usable before approximately the early 1950s. (You may recall that Pareto's speculations were based on fiscal data, whereas Simon Kuznets had hardly a dozen surveys to draw upon—even as late as 1955.)

For developing countries the situation is even worse; very often there is nothing before the 1970s or even the 1980s. This is particularly true for African nations, where household surveys developed, often with the assistance of international organizations, only in the 1980s.[23] What about the two most populous countries in the world? In India comprehensive surveys started in 1952 and have followed more or less the same framework to this day. In China the first existing survey dates from after the Cultural Revolution, in 1978, but the first usable one is from 1980. Moreover, not all countries field surveys annually; some have surveys only once every two years and others even less frequently, once every five years. What does it all mean? First, we would find it very hard, except for the group of advanced and rich economies, to draw a series of yearly inequality statistics based on household surveys. Second, for most countries, we shall be able to say something about inequality starting only with the 1960s, 1970s, or 1980s, and even then with large annual gaps.

Household surveys collect many data, but the ones in which we are interested are the data on income and consumption. Each household is regarded as an "income" or "consumption" unit, and all members of a household are regarded as equally sharing in income or consumption. How do we determine what is the true income of a household member? We take the household's total annual income (adding up the contributions of each member) and divide it by the number of people who lived in the household during that year. This gives us the household per capita income, and it is a key concept because its amount will allow us to rank households and individuals and to decide which of them may be considered poor and which rich.[24]

Why do we insist on using a *per capita* measure? There is a philosophical and a practical argument. The philosophical argument is that we ought to treat each individual equally. If we treated each *household* equally, then people in very large households would individually matter much less than those in small households. If the weight—importance given in calculations—of each household is 1, then my implicit individual weight in a four-member household would be ¼, but my individual weight in a two-member household would be ½. The practical argument is that inequality measures based on households' total and not per capita income would be misleading. The reason is simple. Consider two households with the same overall income, one with two members, another with ten. Which one, do you think, is better off? The answer is obvious.

For simplicity, we generally speak of income distribution, even when the data come in the form of consumption. But the two are not equivalent. Almost always, the data based on income will show greater inequality over a given group of households than the data based on consumption. There are two simple reasons for this. First, there may be people with zero annual income who, for example, finance their current spending out of previously accumulated savings. (Think of students who finance their study years from savings made while they were working.) There are, obviously, no people with zero annual consumption. This makes the distribution according to income more "elongated" around the bottom and thus more unequal (the consumption distribution will be "truncated" at some minimum amount necessary to survive). Second, a similar thing happens at the other end of the distribution. There are many income-rich people who save a part of their income. Thus, their income is greater than their consumption. The high end of the distribution would be also more elongated in the case of income. The measures of inequality will therefore show higher values when we use income as our yardstick than when we use consumption.

Once we have the data on household income, how do we measure inequality? It is not an easy question. Contrast the measurement of inequality with the measurement of national income or gross domestic product. GDP simply adds up incomes made by all people of a nation within a year: We add all wages to all profits to all interest paid out, and so on. Finally, we get one total number. When that number is divided by the total number of inhabitants of a country, we obtain GDP per capita.

But income distribution is composed of many people's incomes, which we do not want simply to add up but rather to compare to each other and yet to express such multiple comparisons in a single number—which would well reflect the diversity of the distribution. That's where the difficulty begins. Any single number that would represent the diversity between incomes such as 1, 5, 15, 2,009, and 34,564 will be somewhat arbitrary. We can, for example, just use the ratio between the largest and smallest numbers (34,564 divided by 1) to depict inequality, but that would leave out everything that happens in the middle. Would not, for example, a distribution such as 1, 400, 620, 1,009, and 34,564 be considered more equal? We can measure inequality by looking at the share of the top only; in this case we would divide 34,564 by the sum of all incomes (1+5+15+2,009+34,564 or 1+400+620+1,009+34,564).[25] This is what a measure of inequality—the top income share—does. The number of options is practically limitless.

One way to reduce the number of options is to proclaim as a desirable property that the measure of inequality should utilize information about all individuals who are part of a given distribution. That means that information about an income of 1 as well as an income of 5 and right up to the top income of 34,564 should all be taken into account. One such, and by far the most popular, measure of inequality is called the Gini coefficient, named after Corrado Gini, the Italian statistician and economist who defined it in 1914 and whose life partly overlapped with Pareto's.[26] The Gini coefficient compares the income of each person with the incomes of all other people individually, and the sum of all such bilateral income differences is divided in turn by the number of people who are included in this calculation and the average income of the group. The ultimate result is such that the Gini coefficient ranges from 0 (where all individuals have the same income and there is no inequality) to 1 (where the entire income of a community is received by one individual). This is a very convenient feature: The coefficient is "bounded from above"; 1 is the maximum possible inequality. Thus, we now have a reliable and useful way of comparing different levels of inequality.

Ginis of either 0 or 1 are equally unrealistic: There are no countries where all people are paid equally, nor are there countries where only one person appropriates the entire income (all the others would have to die from starvation). In real life, Ginis range from about 0.25–0.3 for the most egalitarian countries, such as the Nordic countries and the Czech Republic and Slovakia in central Europe, to 0.6 for the most inegalitarian countries, such as Brazil and South Africa. Oftentimes, for simplicity, Ginis would be presented in percentages; thus, instead of saying Country X's inequality is 0.43, we would say that the inequality is 43 Gini points. We shall stick to this convention throughout the book.

Where is the United States in that range? It is among the most unequal developed countries. Whereas most European Union countries individually (but see Vignette 3.3 for how they look collectively) have Ginis in the range of 30–35, the American Gini is above 40. That has not always been the case. U.S. inequality reached its trough in the late 1970s when the Gini dropped to about 35.[27] After that, during the four pre-Obama presidencies (under Reagan, Bush Sr., Clinton, and Bush Jr.), the U.S. Gini continued to rise, reaching its current level. This was a big increase, as everyone who has lived during that period in the United States knows. Because the Gini is a sluggish measure, even 1–2 Gini-point increases annually are a big deal. Normally—that is, when there is no sustained rise or decline of inequality—the annual movements up and down are within 1 Gini point.

How about other countries? The proverbially egalitarian Sweden has a Gini around 30; Russia, recovering from its communist years and beset by oligarchs, has a Gini in excess of 40. So does China. Both Russia's and China's inequalities have—like the inequality in the United States—sharply increased in the past two decades. Latin America is seldom below 50 Gini points, and so is Africa. Asia is generally unequal although not uniformly so. Japan, South Korea, and Taiwan seem a bit more equal, while Malaysia's and the Philippines' Ginis are at the Latin American levels. If we want to rank regions by how unequal the countries in each of them are, we could say that the top belongs to Latin America, closely followed by Africa, then by Asia, and the least unequal are the rich countries and the postcommunist nations, with the notable exceptions of a couple of relatively high-inequality countries, the United States and Russia.

Or, from a different perspective, we can note that four large economico-political areas, the United States, the European Union, Russia, and China, all (uncannily) exhibit about the same level of inequality: Their Ginis are around or slightly above 40. The differences and similarities between the first two are examined in Vignette 3.3; the specifics of the Russian income distribution are reviewed in Vignettes 1.4, 1.5, and 1.8; and China and her future are discussed in Vignette 1.9.

We can decompose Gini numbers to figure out inequality due to differences in mean incomes between the constituent parts of an area (called the "between-component") and the inequality caused by variation in personal incomes within each constituent part of that area (the "within-component"). Take, for example, the European Union or the United States and their component parts, respectively, countries like Spain and France, or states like Maine and Oregon; or a nation like China and its provinces of Sichuan, Yunnan, Hunan, and so on; or a smaller country like Italy and its administrative regions of Lombardy, Liguria, and Sicily. The interpretation of the between-component is simple: If it is large, then most of the inequality is due to the fact that the area we study is composed of poor and rich parts. If the share of the within-component is high, then geographical inequalities between the different parts of the area must be small, but each part must be composed of very diverse, that is, both rich and poor, people. Consider this approach applied to global inequality: The between-component would relate to inequality due to differences in mean incomes between nations and the within-component to inequality in personal incomes within each nation. We shall use this decomposition frequently (for example, in Vignettes 1.8, 1.9, 3.2, and 3.3) because it is a very powerful tool that lets us look at what lies behind the inequality we measure. This is important because the political implications of one or another type of inequality are indeed very different.

Romance and Riches

It is a truth universally acknowledged that Jane Austen's *Pride and Prejudice* is a novel about love. It is less universally acknowledged that it is a novel about money, too.[1]

The date of the story is not explicitly given in the book, and Jane Austen's world, being intentionally microcosmic and timeless, does not let in a single ray of external events that would allow us to put an unambiguous date on it. Perhaps it was her objective to illustrate how eternal affairs of the heart (and money) are.

The circumstantial evidence, however, points to the stage being set during the Napoleonic Wars, that is, around 1810–1815. The main protagonist is the delightful Elizabeth Bennet, second oldest of five daughters from a rich family headed by Mr. Bennet (the paterfamilias's first name never appears in the book, his own wife calling him Mr. Bennet). Elizabeth and her family live the charmed life of English country gentry, a sort of pleasant idleness punctuated by balls and parties—and the social gossip to which the balls and parties give rise. Elizabeth is beautiful, intelligent, and, of course, unmarried. Her family's annual income is around £3,000, which, divided by seven family members (five sisters and their parents), gives a per capita income of £430 (excluding, as in the rest of the examples here, the imputed value of housing, which must have been considerable). This level of income places the Bennets in the top 1 percent of the English income distribution at the time, as calculated from Robert Colquhoun's English social table done for the early years of the nineteenth century.[2]

Elizabeth meets a rich suitor, Mr. Darcy, whose annual income is put (by all concerned in the book) at £10,000.[3] Both he and his somewhat less rich friend Mr. Bingley are understandably deemed very desirable bachelors by the socially conscious (and no-nonsense) mother of Elizabeth Bennet. Mr. Darcy's huge income places him, at the least, in the top one-tenth of 1 percent of income distribution. Note the huge gap existing between the top 1 percent and the top one-tenth of 1 percent, or, to use George W. Bush's modern phraseology, between "the haves and the have-mores." Although these early-nineteenth-century English haves and have-mores freely intermingle socially (and apparently intermarry), Mr. Darcy's income is more than three times greater than Elizabeth's father's; translated in per capita terms (since Mr. Darcy does not take care of anyone but himself), the ratio is in excess of twenty to one.

It will not be giving away the plot to point out that Elizabeth does have some doubts about the suitability of Mr. Darcy, who, in no uncertain terms, expresses his "adoration"—a period euphemism that would be stated quite differently in a modern book. But rebuffing him forever has an additional unpleasant implication. Due to English inheritance laws, if Mr. Bennet dies without a direct male heir, the house and well-functioning estate revert to his obnoxious cousin, the Reverend William Collins. In that case, Elizabeth has to live on her own income, which is basically her share of the £5,000 that her mother brought ("settled") into the marriage. Elizabeth's independent wealth is thus somewhat indelicately estimated by Reverend Collins, who also doubles as her ill-starred suitor, at £1,000. Mr. Collins assumes that she would make a return of 4 percent on it, and hence earn £40 per year. This is a rather measly amount, approximately equal to twice the mean income in England at the time. It is an income that a family of a surveyor or merchant marine seaman could expect.[4]

This is where the love-wealth trade-off makes its appearance. Consider the situation from the point of view of Elizabeth's mother, worried about the happiness of her daughter. On the one hand, Elizabeth can marry Mr. Darcy and enjoy an annual income of £5,000 (we assume that she contributes nothing in monetary terms to Mr. Darcy and that Mr. Darcy shares his income evenly with Elizabeth). On the other, she can fall into what certainly seems to Mrs. Bennet a world of unremitting poverty, living on less than £50 annually. The income ratio between these two outcomes is simply staggering: more than one hundred to one. At that cost, the alternative of not marrying, or perhaps waiting until an ideal lover appears on the horizon, is out of the question. One would really have to hate Mr. Darcy to reject the deal he is tacitly offering!

But, we may ask, is it any different today? To reset *Pride and Prejudice* in today's United Kingdom, we need simply to look at today's income distribution. After taxes, people in the top 0.1 percent in 2004 made about £400,000 annually per capita, and those in the top 1 percent earned on average £81,000, while the average British per capita income was £11,600. The cost of turning down a Mr. Darcy–equivalent today would still be significant but much less overwhelming: The ratio between the incomes of those in the top 0.1 percent of the distribution and those at twice the mean is about seventeen to one rather than one hundred to one.

Jane Austen has thus not only illustrated the all too common trade-off between romance and riches but also allowed us to see that although the trade-off itself may be timeless, the stakes do vary with time and with the income distribution of the society in which one lives. In more equal societies, we expect that when decisions about marriage are made, love tends to trump wealth more often. And the reverse will then be true in very unequal societies. Will love in very unequal societies, then, exist only outside marriage? To this question we turn next.

Vignette 1.2

Anna Vronskaya?

Every unhappy family is unhappy in its own way.[1] But were Alexei Aleksandrovich Karenin and Anna really so unique?

Anna Karenina is, of course, the story of a married woman who falls in love with a dashing, elegant, and immensely rich younger man, Count Vronsky. It is, at some level, also a critique of social norms and social hypocrisy, because were it not for such "proprieties," Anna would not have been socially ostracized for her relationship with Vronsky and would have found it easier to obtain a divorce (although it is not clear whether she really wanted a divorce since she would have lost the custody of her son). If Anna and Vronsky were to marry, we cannot discard the possibility that theirs would have been a happy marriage—or, to paraphrase Tolstoy's famous opening sentence, one of many identical (happy) marriages. Or perhaps not. For Tolstoy's artistry lies in showing us that it is not solely society and its norms that prevent a happy union of Anna and the count but also their own personalities.

The story of Anna Karenina takes place around 1875 in Moscow, St. Petersburg, and the surrounding countryside. It is contemporaneous with Tolstoy's own life (the novel was published in 1877). Putting it in the roughest possible terms, it describes Anna Karenina's unhappy marriage to the stern, unemotional, high-ranking civil servant Mr. Karenin and her love affair with Mr. Vronsky. That love, at first secret, then in the open, at first full of excitement and promise, later filled with strife, falsehood, and despair, destroys Vronsky's career and leads to a painful, unhappy ending for both of them.

At first blush, *Anna Karenina* and *Pride and Prejudice* have little in common. If one were to compare them by their "chemistry" or "atmospherics," the climate of *Pride and Prejudice* would be that of fickle English summers where brilliant sunshine alternates with dark and menacing clouds. But dark clouds and showers pass as quickly as they appear, and overall one keeps in memory the impression of summery brightness. In contrast, *Anna Karenina* begins like those glorious, warm continental Russian summers where nature seems to explode in front of one's own eyes, moving gradually toward a gloomy fall and ending with a long, dark, bleak, and unremitting winter. The overall atmosphere we take from it is thus much more wintry than summery. As in the cold days of mid-December, it is only with difficulty that we can conjure in our minds the insouciance of summers past.

But, in one respect, with which we are interested here—namely, inequality of incomes and positions—*Anna Karenina* is similar to *Pride and Prejudice*. Consider the starting point of the heroine in both novels: She lives in a very rich, comfortable, and respectable household. In one case, she is married, in the other single. But then in both cases, the next step, love or marriage, is to take her to a much higher level of wealth. Mr. Karenin's income is not mentioned anywhere in the book. However, from his conversation with Anna's brother, Stepan Oblonsky, we find out that he considers 10,000 rubles a very high income, an income, as we find elsewhere in the book, earned by bank directors.[2] We also know that a high government salary amounts to 3,000 rubles and that Stepan Oblonsky, also in the employ of the government, but at a lower level than Mr. Karenin, is making 6,000 rubles.[3] So we can surmise, given Mr. Karenin's very prominent governmental position, that his income is along the order of 8,000–9,000 rubles per year. Now, how about the rich Count Vronsky? For him too, not unlike Mr. Darcy, "everybody" agrees what his income is: 100,000 rubles per year. However, we learn later that, yes, this is the income he should have normally expected, had he not given away one-half of his inheritance to his younger brother. So Vronsky's real income when he meets Anna is only about 50,000 rubles.[4] Afterward, faced with money problems, when he seems to have "recaptured" his own half of the inheritance that he rashly promised to his brother, Vronsky's income probably goes back to its "normal" level of 100,000 rubles.[5]

Let us now look at the wealth jump that would have resulted from Anna's marriage to Vronsky. From a per capita income of around 3,000 rubles (her husband's probable income divided between the couple and their son) to an income level of more than 30,000 rubles per person (again assuming that her monetary contribution, like that of Elizabeth Bennet, is nil, and that Mr. Vronsky, like Mr. Darcy, shares his income evenly with her and their daughter).[6] Thus, the jump from Anna's already plush existence in the large, semipalatial home of the Karenins where she is surrounded by maids, menservants, and nannies to the almost princely lifestyle of Vronsky involves a ten-to-one income multiplication.

For Russia, we lack social tables that would allow us to locate Messrs. Vronsky and Karenin in the income distribution of the time. But there is no doubt that the Karenins belong to the very top of the income ladder (perhaps the top 1 percent), and thus

Mr. Vronsky—again like Mr. Darcy—must be part of the crème de la crème, belonging perhaps to the top one-tenth of 1 percent or even higher. Notice again the huge distance that separates the rich from the exceedingly rich.

But what is the downside for Anna Karenina? Can we see that (lower) side of the income distribution, too? For Anna, the income distribution's downside lies in the past. We learn that she comes from a very modest family,[7] probably living on about a couple hundred rubles per capita annually.[8] Her marriage to Mr. Karenin was socially advantageous, leading to something like a fifteenfold improvement in her standard of living. Another marriage, this time to Mr. Vronsky, would have, as we have just seen, multiplied her income anew by a factor of ten. By virtue of two weddings—that is, in going from around the mean of the income distribution to its very top—Anna would have raised her standard of living by about 150 times (15 x 10).

Are things in Russia better today? Yes. Using household survey data for 2005, we find that the average per capita income among the top 1 percent of Russian households was 340,000 rubles, which is about six and a half times greater than the mean. In 1875 we estimated the ratio between the same two positions in the income distribution to have been fifteen to one (Mr. Karenin's family income versus the mean). So the range of incomes has shrunk in Russia, too. Another Anna who would "travel" across the top part of the income distribution in Russia today would for sure (witness Roman Abramovich) be taken very far from her starting point, but despite the Russian billionaires' riches on which we are often focused, the income gain implicit in that journey would still be less than when Leo Tolstoy wrote his famous novel.

Who Was the Richest Person Ever?

Comparing incomes from the past with those of the present is not easy. We do not have an exchange rate that would convert Roman sesterces or asses or Castellan seventeenth-century pesos into dollars of equal purchasing power today. Even more, what "equal purchasing power" might mean in that case is far from clear. "Equal purchasing power" should mean that one is able to buy with X Roman sesterces the same bundle of goods and services as with Y U.S. dollars today. But not only have the bundles changed (no DVDs in Roman times), but were we to constrain the bundle to cover only the goods that existed both then and now, we would soon find that the relative prices have changed substantially. Services then were relatively cheap (because wages were low); nowadays, services in rich countries are expensive. The reverse would be true for bread or olive oil.

Thus, to compare the wealth and income of the *richissime* in several historical periods, the most reasonable approach is to situate them in their historical context and measure their economic power in terms of their ability to purchase human labor (of average skill) at that time and place. In some sense, a given quantum of human labor is a universal numeraire, a yardstick with which we measure welfare. As Adam Smith wrote more than two hundred years ago, "[A person] must be rich or poor according to the quantity of labor which he can command."[1] Moreover, this quantum embodies improvements in productivity and welfare over time, since the income of somebody like Bill Gates today will be measured against the average incomes of people who presently live in the United States.

A natural place to start is ancient Rome, for which we have data on the extremely wealthy individuals and whose economy was sufficiently "modern" and monetized to make comparisons with the present or more recent past meaningful. We can consider three individuals from the classic Roman age. The fabulously rich triumvir Marcus Crassus's fortune was estimated around the year 50 BCE at some 200 million sesterces (HS).[2] The emperor Octavian Augustus's imperial household fortune was estimated at 250 million HS around the year 14 CE.[3] Finally, the enormously rich freedman Marcus Antonius Pallas (under Nero) is thought to have been worth 300 million HS in the year 52.[4]

Take Crassus, who has remained associated with extravagant affluence (not to be confused, though, with the Greek king Croesus, whose name has become eponymous with wealth). With 200 million sesterces and an average annual interest rate of 6 percent (which was considered a "normal" interest rate in the Roman "golden age," that is, before the inflation of the third century), Crassus's annual income could be estimated at 12 million HS. The mean income of Roman citizens around the time of Octavian's death (14 CE) is thought to have been about 380 sesterces per annum and we can assume that it was about the same sixty years earlier, when Crassus lived.[5] Thus expressed, Crassus's income was equal to the annual incomes of about 32,000 people, a crowd that would fill about half of the Colosseum.[6]

Let us fast-forward more closely to the present and apply the same reasoning to three American wealth icons: Andrew Carnegie,

John D. Rockefeller, and Bill Gates. Carnegie's fortune reached its peak in 1901 when he purchased U.S. Steel. His share in U.S. Steel was $225 million. Applying the same return of 6 percent, and using U.S. GDP per capita (in 1901 prices) of $282, allows us to conclude that Carnegie's income exceeded that of Crassus. With his annual income Carnegie could have purchased the labor of almost 48,000 people at the time without making any dent in his fortune. (Notice that in all these calculations, we assume that the wealth of the *richissime* individual remains intact. He simply uses his annual income, that is, yield from his wealth, to purchase labor.)

An equivalent calculation for Rockefeller, taking his wealth at its 1937 peak ($1.4 billion),[7] yields Rockefeller's income to be equal to that of about 116,000 people in the United States in the year 1937. Thus, Rockefeller was almost four times as rich as Crassus and more than twice as rich as Andrew Carnegie. The people whom he could hire would easily fill Pasadena's Rose Bowl, and even quite a few would have remained outside the gates.

How does Bill Gates fare in this kind of comparison? Bill Gates's fortune in 2005 was put by *Forbes* at $50 billion. Income could then be estimated at $3 billion annually, and since the U.S. GDP per capita in 2005 was about $40,000, Bill Gates could, with his income, command about 75,000 workers. This places him somewhere between Andrew Carnegie and John D. Rockefeller, but much above the "poor" Marcus Crassus.

But this calculation leaves open the question of how to treat billionaires such as the Russian Mikhail Khodorovsky and Mexican Carlos Slim who are both "global" and "national." Khodorovsky's wealth, at the time when he was the richest man in Russia in 2003, was estimated at $24 billion.[8] Globally speaking, he was much less rich than Bill Gates. Yet if we assess his fortune locally and again use the same assumptions as before, he was able to buy more than a quarter million annual units of labor, at their average price. In other words, contrasted with the relatively low incomes of his countrymen, Mikhail Khodorovsky was richer, and potentially more powerful, than Rockefeller in the United States in 1937. It is probably this latter fact—the potential political power—that brought him to the attention of the Kremlin.

Without touching a penny of his wealth, Khodorovsky could, if need be, create an army of a quarter-million people. He was negotiating with both the Americans and the Chinese, almost as a state would, the construction of new gas and oil pipelines. Such potential power met its nemesis in his downfall and eventual jailing. However, Russian history being what it is, the shortest way between two stints in power often takes one through a detour in Siberia. We might not have seen the last of Mr. Khodorovsky.

The Mexican Carlos Slim does Khodorovsky one better. His wealth, also according to *Forbes* magazine, prior to the global financial crisis in 2009, was estimated at more than $53 billion. Using the same calculation as before, we find that Slim could command even more labor than Khodorovsky at his peak: some 440,000 Mexicans. So he appears to have been, locally, the richest of all! No stadium in Mexico, not even the famous Azteca, would come close to accommodating all the compatriots Mr. Slim could hire with his annual income.

Another complication that may be introduced is the size of populations. When Crassus lived and commanded the labor incomes of 32,000 people, this represented 1 out of each 1,500 people living in the Roman Empire at the time. Rockefeller's 116,000 Americans were a higher proportion of the U.S. population: 1 person out of each 1,100 people. Thus, in both respects Rockefeller beats Crassus.

Can we then say who was the richest of them all? Since the wealthy also tend to go "global" and measure their wealth against the wealth of other rich people living in different countries, it was probably Rockefeller who was the richest of all because he was able to command the highest number of labor units in the then richest country in the world. But when the *richissime* decide to play a political role in their own countries (which may not be the richest countries in the world, such as, for example, Russia and Mexico), then their power there may exceed even the power of the most globally rich.

How Unequal Was the Roman Empire?

We do have an implicit theory about income inequality in preindustrial economies. Kuznets' hypothesis (see Essay I and Vignette 1.10), formulated in 1955, the bread-and-butter of inequality economics, posits that inequality charts an inverted U shape as the economy transforms from predominantly agricultural to predominantly industrialized or "modern." Inequality is therefore supposed to emerge only when societies enter a sustained process of modernization, and thus inequality in preindustrial societies, including even the most sophisticated among them, like the Roman Empire, should be low. But in contrast to this view, we also have an image of preindustrial societies as combining abject poverty in the bottom with extravagant wealth on the top. Could both these images be right? As we shall see below, yes—and this is one of the key features that distinguishes inequality in premodern times from inequality in modern times.

Let us start with the sketch of the social structure as it existed during the early Empire. We have in mind here the period that spans the first two centuries of the Christian era: approximately from the accession to power of Octavian (later called Augustus) in year 31 BCE to the end of the rule of the "five good emperors" that coincides with the arrival to power of Commodus, Marcus

Aurelius's son, in the year 180 CE. This also marks the beginning of what Gibbon famously pronounced as the "decline" of Rome.

At the top of the early Empire was, of course, the emperor—both politically and, to a large extent, financially. How rich was the emperor or, more exactly, he and his family? It was estimated that the annual income of Octavian Augustus's household was 15 million sesterces (HS), which amounted to about 0.08 percent of the total income of the entire Empire (composed in those days of 50–55 million people).[1] This is, in relative terms, about eight times as much as the share of King George III of England in the beginning of the nineteenth century.[2] (Incidentally, George III was the British king during the period in which *Pride and Prejudice* takes place; see Vignette 1.1.) Augustus's posthumous donative to people, paid out of private and public funds combined, was put by the famous Roman historian Cornelius Tacitus at 43.5 million sesterces,[3] which was approximately 0.2 percent of the Empire's GDP at that time. This is about the same as if George W. Bush had, upon leaving office, granted from his private purse some $30 billion to distribute among the citizenry.

Nor was Augustus's largesse unique. In the year 33, Tiberius (who succeeded Augustus) gave about 0.5 percent of the GDP (equivalent to $75 billion in today's U.S. income) to solve the banking liquidity crisis—very much like what the U.S. Treasury did in 2009. Tacitus's text has an uncannily modern ring to it, except that it is an individual rather than the whole government that provides the money:

> The decree requiring land purchases and sales . . . had the
> opposite effect since when the capitalists received payments

they hoarded it, to buy land at their convenience. These extensive transactions reduced prices. But large-scale debtors found it difficult to sell; so many of them were ejected from their properties, and lost not only their estates but their rank and reputation. Then Tiberius came to the rescue. He distributed a hundred million sesterces among especially established banks, for interest-free three-year state loans, against the security of double the value in landed property. Credit was thus restored; and gradually private lenders reappeared.[4]

In the year 36 Tiberius distributed as much to compensate the losses of those who suffered from a large fire in Rome.[5] Nero continued this practice. In his earlier book *The Histories*, Tacitus estimated the total of donatives during Nero's reign of fourteen years to have amounted to 2.32 billion HS, which was about 10 percent of the annual GDP. Where did all the money come from? Was it private or public? Did the emperors make a sharp distinction between the two? Probably not. Greco-Roman historian Cassius Dio describes Octavian's treatment of public and private funds: "nominally the public revenues had been separated from his own, but in practice the former, too, were spent as he saw fit."[6] As one of the most eminent Roman historians, Walter Scheidel from Stanford, says, emperors' behavior was probably similar to the way today's Saudi rulers or Saddam Hussein treat private and public purses.[7]

No doubt about one thing: The emperors were extremely rich. But they were not the only rich people in the Empire. A lot of wealth came from the administration and plunder of provinces; in a metaphor by the famous English economist Alfred Marshall, "it was dug by the sword, not the spade."[8] We have already seen (in Vignette 1.3) that probably the richest man in the history of the Roman Empire was not an emperor. Rome was a plutocratic society where class segmentation was based on a combination of holding a hereditary title and having huge current wealth. To make sure that both conditions were fulfilled, there were explicit censuses (wealth qualifications) for the top three classes: senators, the equestrian order (the knights), and decurions (or municipal senators). The first two classes resided in Rome (or in the rest of Italy); the third one was, as the name indicates, dispersed across the Empire. The census for senators was, at the time of the early Empire, 1 million sesterces (HS); that for the knights was 250,000 HS. To put these numbers in perspective, we need to take into account, for example, that the average wealth of a senator was probably around 3 million HS, which, using a conventional rate of interest of 6 percent per annum, gives an income of about 180,000 HS. This is about five hundred times more than the estimated average Roman income at that time. Casting this again in current U.S. terms, senators would be people with an *income* (not wealth!) of about $21 million annually.[9] Today's U.S. senators are comparatively poor: Their annual salary is less than $200,000, and their average net wealth is estimated at about $9 million.[10] Assuming a 6 percent return on their wealth and adding it to the salaries would still make their average income less than $700,000, a fraction of that of their Roman peers.

The number of Roman senators was, however, small (perhaps about 600), while the equestrian order might have numbered 40,000. The data get much more uncertain for the decurions because the wealth requirements differed from city to city (depending on local wealth), and a calculation that adds all the municipal senators across the Empire heavily depends on our estimates of the number of cities, the sizes of the municipal senates, and so forth. But to give an overall idea of their number, we can note that it was assessed at between 130,000 and 360,000 people. In any case, adding the three richest classes together yields between less than 200,000 and 400,000 people. The top of the pyramid was, as we can see, rather small if we remember that there were 50–55 million inhabitants. The top represented less than 1 percent of the total population.[11]

Not surprisingly, the vast majority of people lived at a very low income: subsistence or just above the subsistence level. The gradient (how fast income increases as we move from poorer to richer income classes) was much flatter than in modern societies. Percentage differences in income among this vast mass of people were small. Thus, the income gradient was flat up to a very high point in income distribution. But then, and quickly, as we approach the very top of the distribution, the gradient would suddenly increase, much more so than in modern societies. Thus, unlike a modern society that is characterized by a steady increase of the gradient, in Rome the middle was not much different from the bottom. There was a dearth—although not a total absence—of people whom we would call (using modern terminology) the "middle class."

We can thus see why both of our preconceived notions—of generalized equality and drastic income disparity among the ancients—are true: They just refer to different parts of the income distribution. The first notion (equality in poverty) is validated when we look at the income gradient along most of the distribution or at standard measures of income inequality. They are summary measures that take into account the income of everybody in a society; now, since most people's incomes were not very different from each other, such inequality statistics cannot be very high, either. In terms of our favorite measure of inequality, the Gini coefficient (see Essay I), inequality in the early Roman Empire was estimated to have been around 41–42 points.[12] This is the level that is almost exactly the same as in the United States today and in the enlarged European Union (see also Vignette 3.3). But the second notion (vast wealth amid pervasive misery) is validated too if we look at the extremes of the distribution. The yawning gap between the two extremes was much larger than anything we observe today.

There were also large spatial inequalities. During the period under consideration here, the Roman Empire, governed from a single center, extended over an enormous territory, running from today's Morocco and Spain in the west to the easternmost reaches of today's Turkey and Armenia. Along the north-south axis, it went from England to the Persian Gulf (although only under Trajan, who ruled from 98 to 117; the Empire receded from the Gulf later). It covered 3.4 million square kilometers, which is about three-quarters of the area of the continental United States. Over that landmass lived some 50–55 million people (the density thus being only about one-fifth of that of the United States today) at different levels of development and income. Economic historian Angus Maddison estimates the range of regional incomes.[13] Peninsular Italy was the richest, some 50 percent above the Empire-wide average. It was followed by Egypt (the granary of the Empire), also slightly richer than the Empire-wide mean. Then came Greece, Asia Minor, parts of Africa (Libya and today's Tunisia), southern Spain (approximately today's Andalusia), and southern France (approximately today's Provence). The differences among the still poorer regions were small: The islands (Sicily, Sardinia, and Corsica) might have been just slightly better off than Gaul, North Africa (today's Algeria and Morocco) came next, and at the very end were the eastern (Danubian) provinces. The income ratio between the richest and the poorest regions was relatively low: about two to one.[14]

If one looks at today's incomes of the areas that were part of the early Roman Empire, it is immediately apparent that the differences are much greater now. At the top today are Switzerland, Austria, Belgium, and France with GDPs per capita around $PPP 35,000.[15] At the other extreme, Tunisia and Algeria have GDPs per capita of some $PPP 7,000–8,000 (and Balkan countries are only slightly better off). Thus, today's top-to-bottom "provincial" ratio over the same territories has risen to five to one. Moreover, the pecking order of "provinces" has changed, too. Broadly speaking, the South was then richer than the North; today, it is the opposite. However, the advantage of the West compared to the East of Europe has remained.

Was Socialism Egalitarian?

A short answer to the question posed in the title is, yes, socialism was egalitarian.[1] We know that not only because the transition to market economy has led to (at times) huge increases in inequality in the formerly socialist countries but also from the comparative studies of inequality in socialism and capitalism while the former still existed. It became a custom, in Kuznets-type regressions that charted inequality as a function of income levels (see Essay I and Vignette 1.10), to use for socialist countries, in addition to income, a dummy variable, that is, a specific variable that takes only values of 0 or 1 (1 if a country is socialist, 0 otherwise) and to expect that the coefficient on this variable would carry a negative sign—indicating that everything else being the same, the very fact that a country is socialist would imply a lower level of inequality.[2]

Four questions are important in this respect: How much was socialism more equal than a corresponding capitalist society? How was this achieved? Was it worth it? And what type of inequalities existed under socialism?

The value of the Gini coefficient for socialist countries was in the upper 20s or lower 30s (see Essay I for the empirical values of the Gini coefficient). These are some of the lowest values registered after the end of World War II when measurement of inequality became standard in most countries in the world.

Approximately speaking, socialism was some 6–7 Gini points more equal than capitalism, with European capitalist countries such as West Germany, France, Italy, and Denmark having at the time (1970s and 1980s) Gini coefficients in the low- to mid-30s range. If we want to put a percentage number on this, we could say that socialism reduced inequality by approximately one-quarter (compared to what it would have been under capitalism). Now, the increases after the transition back to capitalism in the 1990s were often greater: In Russia alone, inequality doubled. However, this inequality under the "new" capitalism of these countries represents probably an "overshoot" compared to what it would have been if they were "normal" capitalist countries. The reasons lie in a very corrupt privatization process that led to immense wealth for some and poverty and unemployment for many, and the fact that the 1990s, much more so than the 1970s or even 1980s, was a "decade of inequality." Inequality rose almost everywhere and was not regarded as negatively as during the heyday of welfare capitalism. So the postcommunist countries just "imitated" their Western counterparts in letting inequality shoot up in the 1990s.

How did socialism realize that greater equality? There were several things, like a package, that led to it. First, nationalization of the means of production and of land (or the agrarian reform in several countries) obliterated the large industrial and landowning fortunes. This was particularly the case in countries like Russia (after the revolution in 1917) and Hungary and Poland (after 1947) where large landholdings still existed. Private industrialists in all countries disappeared, their assets were nationalized, and stock markets were closed. Resource wealth was nationalized as well. Thus, top incomes were severely reduced. Second, full employment cut the bottom of the income distribution as nationalization cut the top. Everybody had a job, and however small the pay (since many of such make-believe jobs were quite unproductive), it was better than not having a job at all. Third, generalized compulsory and free education increased the overall education level of the population, and explicit policies introduced to limit wage spreads between intellectual and physical laborers as well as between the more and less skilled workers reduced the educational premium. Whereas in capitalist societies one additional year of education is generally found to increase one's salary by between 7 and 9 percent, under socialism that percentage was halved.[3] Thus, the wage distribution was much more narrow than under capitalism. Finally, a network of different social transfers, from subsidized transportation and subsidized vacations to child allowances and pensions, which were received more or less by everybody, further leveled incomes. Low wage differentiation and social benefits that were paid simply by virtue of demographic characteristics (e.g., to *all* children, to *all* people older than sixty, and so on) made some economists argue that under socialism one could predict the income of households from their demographic characteristics alone: whether there were two or three children, the age of the parents, whether both husband and wife worked, and so forth.[4] Clearly, if that's the case, then your individual education, effort, skill, and the like are immaterial. They will not increase your family income by a penny.

And therein lay the problem with socialist leveling. It simply took away all, or almost all, incentive to work harder, to learn more. Of course, entrepreneurship was impossible because there was no private property and hence no entrepreneurs as individuals

(such entrepreneurs, if they appeared, would be branded specu-
lators and promptly jailed). But even leaving aside entrepreneurship (after all, hardly any society has more than a couple
percent of such individuals), leveling of incomes took away any
incentive for higher personal productivity. Why work harder if
you get no benefit from it? To be sure, under the early Stalin-
ism, at the launch of the five-year plans, an extreme form of the
piece-rate wage system was used, in a form more extreme than
in American capitalism at the time, with the result that wage
differentials increased. But this was rather an aberration. We are
focused here on the mature and sedate socialism of the 1960–
1989 period.

It is not surprising that the lack of incentives led to a stag-
nating or very slowly rising productivity. Innovations also dried
up. If one could gain nothing from improving the way a product
was made or inventing a new product, why bother? Notice a following fact. Socialist economies, in their fifty to seventy years of
existence, have never produced a single consumer-good product
that was exportable and successful internationally. There was no
socialist brand produced outside of the military and space industrial complex in the Soviet Union. No successful car, or stereo, or
watch, or nicely designed clothing, was ever produced by socialist systems. This is quite extraordinary since "reverse engineering" of (say) Western-produced cars and, consequently, the
production of at least equally good cars should not be thought
an impossible task for a centralized government that could put a
lot of resources into whatever it chose. But not even East Germany (technologically the most advanced socialist country) came
up with anything better than a Trabant or a Wartburg, sad copies
of West German cars. So if the lack of incentives for hard work

and innovation was one of the key reasons socialism stagnated and collapsed, one may legitimately wonder whether so much equality was worth it.

What were the socialist inequalities? They were political in origin. Those who were "more equal" than others had important political functions. They were high up in the Communist Party or state hierarchy (the two being interchangeable), directors of large enterprises, state poet laureates, highly decorated military or police, and so on. But in order to be somebody at whatever position, you also had to be relatively high in the Communist Party, since the top jobs were distributed only among that group of people. The group, however, should not be viewed as some medieval caste; rather, think of it as a kind of bureaucratic meritocracy— upward and downward mobility in Communist Parties having been quite high. Yugoslav communist leader, later turned (of his own volition) dissident, Milovan Djilas dubbed it already in 1953 "a new class." The term stuck.[5]

But another feature is important when we consider these inequalities. Benefits were strongly linked to particular jobs; they came as ex officio benefits: a large apartment with a minimal rent, free vacations in nice hotels or villas, a government-owned dacha in the countryside, and at very high levels only, a chauffeur-driven car and perhaps even some domestic help (although that was rare). Not much came in the form of higher monetary income. The fact that privileges were attached to jobs was not accidental: This system ensured that job holders would not become independent from the higher-ups in the party or too "freethinking"; unwillingness to toe the party line would quickly lead to demotion, and the latter to a sudden loss of all privileges. Moreover, the fact that the monetary wages even of the top cadre were not much higher than those of ordinary workers or salarymen meant that they could not accumulate much money and have some personal wealth to fall upon after their demotion. Personal wealth serves, as we know, as a bulwark against government arbitrariness and provides the means to exert personal freedom.[6] But if you have no accumulated wealth and all your income and perks are job related, the incentives are really very strong not to create waves.

Another proequality instrument, guaranteed and compulsory full employment, should also be seen in its political context. Similarly to what we just saw, it was used as a political control mechanism. Its origins lay in two interconnected claims: Socialism will eliminate economic cycles (so there would be full employment throughout); and socialism, being a societywide project, requires the participation of all—hence, everybody was supposed to work (and not to idle about) and contribute to the creation of a new society. But some governments, especially the Soviets, used the idea of full employment in a very creative way: A dissident would be fired from his or her job, not given any other, and then imprisoned for what was called "vagrancy" or "parasitism"—that is, unwillingness to contribute to "socialist construction."[7]

Although empirical studies invariably find inequality to have been low in socialism, the perception of many people who lived under that regime, and of many Western observers, is that inequalities between the top and the "rest" were huge. This is based on two things. First, those at the top (and close to the top) of political hierarchy often had access to goods that were in short supply. Thus, if most of the population had to wait in lines to get meat, or run from one store to another to find butter and cooking oil, a steady delivery of these goods (sometimes even imported) would seem to be a huge luxury even if their objective value was quite limited. Second, there was a deep contradiction—which did not go unnoticed by the people and deeply irked both those who were opponents of the regime as well as those who were the "true" believers in it—between the claims of economic superiority of socialism made by the leaders and the same leaders' unbridled pursuit of Western goods in their everyday life. In no communist country did the political elite drive East German rather than West German cars; they did not wear Bulgarian-made, but rather Italian-made shoes; they were buying not Czech stereo systems, but Japanese. This provided tangible proof that they did not believe what they were saying, and in addition, it exacerbated inequality by making it very obvious—particularly since many such imported goods were virtually impossible to obtain for the majority of the population.

I think there are fewer things that contributed more to the disenchantment of the population in communism than the ostentatious consumption patterns of their leaders. Granted, the value of these consumption goods was trivial compared to the spending patterns of today's oligarchs, or of the rich in the West and Latin America. The communist elite was relatively poor compared to other elites. But the point is that their behavior stood out so sharply because it was so blatantly in contradiction with the ideology they preached.

The rise and fall of communism may be interpreted in many different ways. As far as inequality is concerned, it holds several important lessons. First, it unambiguously disproves Vilfredo Pareto's contention of an "iron law" of income distribution: It shows that distributions can be altered by different political arrangements. Second, it shows that economic leveling (combined with political coercion) leads to stagnation and ultimately decline. Third, it shows that it is important that the elites' behavior not be overtly out of step with the ideological justification of their rule. The financial elite on Wall Street may be well advised to ponder the third lesson.

In What Parisian Arrondissement Should You Live in the Thirteenth Century and Today?

Many people have been charmed by Paris's Sixteenth Arrondissement, its well-maintained buildings, nice restaurants, pleasant small parks, abundance of beautifully laid-out shops, and the general air of affluence.[1] And indeed the French government fiscal data for 2007 show the Sixteenth to be one of the richest arrondissements in Paris. Together with the Sixth, Seventh, and Eighth, it is the arrondissement where per capita fiscal income (that is, income reported to tax authorities) is more than twice as high as the Parisian average.[2] As can be seen on the map on page 65, the dark-shaded rich arrondissements cover the western parts of Paris and straddle the river. On the other end of the spectrum, the poorest arrondissements are at the edge of the northeastern part of Paris: the Eighteenth, Nineteenth, and Twentieth. The fiscal income per person there is less than two-thirds of the Paris-wide average. These few simple numbers allow us to see how big the differences are among the arrondissements: The top-to-bottom ratio is approximately four to one (2.5 divided by less than two-thirds).

Now, the map includes only what is officially called Paris, that is, the twenty arrondissements contained within the city administrative limits (within *le périphérique*), which have not changed in almost two centuries. The suburbs are both richer and much poorer. The leafy suburb of Neuilly (west of Paris) provides one example of the former; the immigrant (often Arab-and African-populated) suburbs, which in 2005 exploded in rioting, provide examples of the latter. Thus, the gap between the richest and poorest parts of Paris, if we were to include the entire metropolitan area of 12 million inhabitants (as opposed to about 2.5 million living within Paris proper), would be much greater.

The richest arrondissements are also the most unequal; the poorest, the most equal. There is pretty much a monotonic relationship: The richer the arrondissement, the greater the inequality within it. This means that the richest arrondissements contain people who are also relatively poor; in other words, the rich arrondissements are fairly heterogeneous. And indeed, if we look at the lowest class according to fiscal income (families in all arrondissements are divided into the same twelve fiscal income classes),[3] we find that it accounts for one-fifth of all families living in the Sixteenth Arrondissement, which is not much different from the share of the same lowest fiscal class in the poor arrondissements. But the difference lies in the share of rich families. About one-fifth of families in rich arrondissements belong to the top (twelfth) fiscal class, while in poor arrondissements the rich families are quasi nonexistent. We can therefore say that in today's Paris, poor families are rather evenly dispersed across the city, but rich families are concentrated in a few arrondissements, and in particular in the Sixteenth, where more than 20 percent of all rich Parisians live, a proportion four times higher than the average.

To follow the changing economic geography of cities over a long time is not easy because the data for the "deep" past are not available. Paris is an exception. We have Parisian fiscal data from the very end of the thirteenth and beginning of the fourteenth centuries. They have recently been digitized and used by University of Jerusalem economic historian Nathan Sussman.[4] Like the 2007 data, the old data are fiscal in origin, too. They provide the average wealth tax paid by each household, or more exactly by each hearth (*foyer*). Applying back the tax rates that were assessed, one can estimate total wealth. For sure, the tax data then were much less reliable than today. They left out a significant portion of the population, particularly the very rich (nobility and clergy), who were exempt from taxation, and the very poor, who had no assets and paid no taxes. In addition, we deal here with the distribution of wealth rather than income, and we know, from numerous studies, that wealth is more unequally distributed than income. Nevertheless, a careful comparison is possible, especially if we use the tax data for 1292, which are more complete than for the other years: They include almost 15,000 households; that is, around 70,000 individuals out of a total Parisian population that was estimated at more than 100,000.[5]

Paris then was much smaller than now and was divided into twenty-four parishes. The map shows the relative incomes of these parishes (as with the arrondissements, the richer parishes are colored in darker hues). The income ratio between the richest parish (St. Jacques), which would be part of the First Arrondissement today, and the poorest parish (St. Marcel), which would today be in the Fifth, was about six to one. It would seem that the top-to-bottom ratio was substantially higher than today, although we need to be very careful on this point because of the two biases that (luckily) just might cancel each other out: The 1292 data refer to wealth that is always more unequally distributed than income; on the other hand, they leave out, as we have seen, the two extremes of the income distribution (the rich nobles and the poor vagrants). The latter bias reduces measured inequality.

The richest parts of Paris were then on the right bank of the Seine and the island of La Cité, whereas the left bank was much poorer. The area that today is the Sixteenth Arrondissement was not part of thirteenth-century Paris. But even a cursory comparison of the two maps shows the changing geography of wealth and poverty. The richest parts "migrated" from the center of Paris and the right bank of the river, much farther west, and crossed the river, thus "carrying" upward with them some parts along the left bank as well. What used to be the poorest parts (generally on the left bank) are nowadays in the middle of the Parisian income distribution and even higher, while the poorest arrondissements became the ones lying relatively far from the center, in the northeastern edge of Paris, which were not even part of the city in 1292.

What explains this geographical migration? According to Monique Pinçon-Charlot and Michel Pinçon, urban researchers at the French Conseil National de la Recherche Scientifique, the explanation is that the western part of Paris became attached to Paris and urbanized relatively late, in the nineteenth century.[6] This was the period of economic upswing during Napoléon III and the ascendant "haute bourgeoisie." They wanted to have much more space and more comfortable apartments and homes, and the western part of Paris, relatively underdeveloped at the time, allowed that. They also preferred to construct their own

DISTRIBUTION OF WEALTH:
PARIS - 13TH CENTURY (BY PARISH)

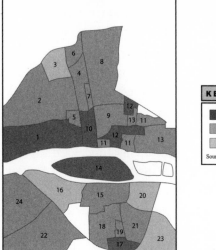

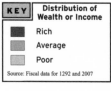

KEY | Distribution of Wealth or Income

■ Rich
■ Average
□ Poor

Source: Fiscal data for 1292 and 2007

DISTRIBUTION OF INCOME:
PARIS - 21ST CENTURY (BY ARRONDISSEMENT)

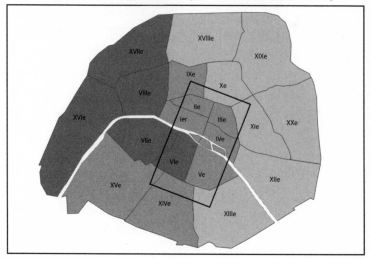

housing rather than do expensive renovation of the often decrepit housing in the cramped downtown Parisian quarters. Further adding to the "western drift," the eastern part of Paris, Faubourg Saint-Antoine, has traditionally been more industrial (having escaped guilds' regulations), and thus was far less attractive. The wealthy therefore slowly reestablished themselves in the western part of Paris, where (as we have just seen) they still remain.

Now, what about the distinction between the left and right banks that seems to have existed for a long time, with the right being the administrative center, with the Court (Le Louvre), ministries, expensive and fashionable merchant streets, and the stock exchange, and the left being the domain of students and religious congregations? This is indeed the picture conveyed by the late-thirteenth-century tax census. It is also the traditional image of Paris, divided by the Seine in two parts that fulfill different functions: grosso modo, the right bank, those of power, commerce, and administration; the left bank, those of the soul and mind. But was it always thus? Not really. That division did not exist in Roman times, in the old Lutetia (the Roman name for today's Paris). While the palace and the temple were situated on the Île de la Cité (Notre Dame stands today close to where a Roman palace was), other important buildings like the arena, theater, baths, and the forum were all on the left bank.[7] No significant part of the city was located on the right bank. We can see it from the description of Paris, written in year 362 by Roman emperor Julian, Constantine the Great's nephew, the man who attempted to slow the Christianization of the Empire and possibly return it to Greco-Roman worship. Julian, who spent several years in Paris as Caesar (a position just a step lower than emperor) and was very fond of the city, thus reminisced of his time there:

> I happened to be in winter quarters at my beloved Lutetia—for that is how the Celts call the capital of the Parisians. It is a small island lying in the river, a wall entirely surrounds it, and wooden bridges lead to it on both sides. The river seldom rises and falls, but usually is of the same depth in the winter as in the summer season. . . . For since the inhabitants live on the island they have to draw their water chiefly from the river. The winter too is rather mild there, perhaps from the warmth of the ocean. . . . And a good kind of vine grows thereabouts, and some persons have even managed to grow fig-leaves by covering them in winter.[8]

And indeed in those early days, the left bank was a better choice since it was less likely to be flooded. The right bank was more marshy, as still conveyed in the name of the famous quarter Le Marais (the Marshes), which had to be drained in the twelfth century before it became available for the construction of housing.

The geography of wealth of Paris thus seems to have mutated from the one that was centered in Roman times at the island in the middle of the Seine (perhaps a natural location to start the construction of the city) and the left bank, to the one concentrated on the right bank during the Middle Ages, and to the current configuration where—if you want to live among the wealthy—your preferred choice should be the western part of Paris.

Who Gains from Fiscal Redistribution?

When we speak of income distribution, we almost invariably have in mind the distribution of what in economics is called "disposable income." As the name says, this is income that remains at the disposition of households to save or spend, after they have paid direct taxes to the government and received from the government cash benefits like social security and unemployment compensation. But there is another income concept that is, at times, useful. This is "market income," which is income received from wages, profits, interest, rent, and so forth, before fisc (that is, before either taxation or receipt of government transfers). Obviously, people with very low market income will be people who either are unable (or unwilling) to sell their labor services and lack property from which they could derive some income. Oftentimes, in developed countries, they are the unemployed. Incidentally, state-funded pensions (like social security) or private pensions are considered equivalent to wage payments (only delayed) and thus included in market income.[1]

Having thus set the stage, this question is often asked: What income groups benefit the most from government redistribution (taxes and cash benefits)? There is a theory that says that in democracies, where people vote on redistributive policies, the main beneficiaries should be people in the middle of (market) income distribution. The rationale is as follows. Suppose there are three people with their market incomes being, respectively, low, medium, and high. (Market income is important here because you decide on tax-and-spend policies you prefer based on the market income you have earned.) The poor person will tend to prefer high tax rates and a lot of government spending because he is likely to benefit from it. For exactly the opposite reason, the rich person will prefer low tax rates. Then the pivotal vote is held by the person in the middle. With whomever he aligns, that side wins two to one. The median voter, or what we may call "the middle-class voter," becomes the decisive voter. We would in principle expect him to gain through the process of redistribution. He may not gain more than the poor because tax rates are generally progressive (that is, they increase as market income goes up), but, for sure, we would expect that the middle-class voter would gain in the process of redistribution since, after all, he chooses the tax rate and the benefits that go with it. That means that he would be better off when measured in terms of disposable than in terms of market income.

Is this the case? As it turns out, not exactly, and not unambiguously.[2] First, we find that it is the poor who gain the most from redistribution. Their income share, which is generally tiny in terms of market income, increases, after government redistribution, to still small but more reasonable. For example, in major democracies studied over the period 1980–2000, the share of the poorest decile (10 percent of the population) in total market income is very small, only 1.2 percent. After government redistribution the income share of these same people rises, on average across countries, to 4.1 percent. The poorest

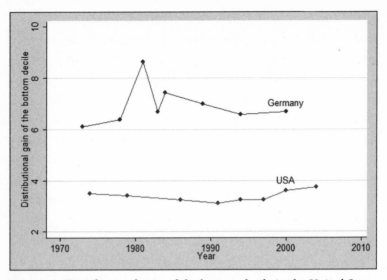

FIGURE 1 Distributional gain of the bottom decile in the United States and Germany

Note: The gain is calculated as we move from market to disposable income.

decile thus gains almost 3 percentage points. The equivalent numbers for the second-poorest decile are 3.6 and 5 percent. The gain here is 1.4 percent. For each successive (richer) decile, the gains diminish, until they turn to be slightly negative for the fifth and sixth deciles, and then, of course, continue to be even more negative for the higher deciles. Gains are not the same in all countries, as Figure 1 illustrates in the examples of the United States and Germany. In the former the bottom decile gains about 4 percentage points (which, as we have seen, is the average for the countries included in the analysis), but the gain is significantly and consistently higher in Germany: around 7 percentage points.

Two conclusions are immediately apparent. First, the biggest beneficiaries of the redistribution process in developed countries are those who "start" the poorest, that is, those with the lowest market income. This is not surprising. What is surprising is that the middle-class deciles (fifth and sixth), whom we expected to gain through redistribution, do not. Their share even decreases slightly. Moreover, this result does not hold only for the developed countries as a whole; it holds for every country individually: The extent of the share *loss* of the middle class varies from country to country, and from year to year, but it is overwhelmingly present.

This opens up a question to which we do not have a good answer: Why, presumably, do the decisive (middle-class) voters vote for a process that, in the end, leaves them with a smaller share of the national income pie than before? There are two possibilities, neither of which we can decisively prove or reject. The first is that the middle-class voter votes for some redistribution policies as potential insurance. Although at the time when we take our snapshot picture of redistribution, he is not receiving anything from such redistribution, he votes for it "just in case." For example, the middle class may accept higher taxation of current incomes in order to fund unemployment benefits in the expectation that, were they to be in need of such benefits, they would be eligible. It is a reasonable hypothesis, but, short of having longitudinal data that follow the same groups of people year after year (so that we can indeed establish whether they eventually gain from these transfers), it is hard to find out if it is true. Moreover, suppose that we find that, even after following these middle-class families throughout their lives, we find that they still lose through redistribution. We can explain that, too: Perhaps voting for unemployment benefits, even if they never receive a penny from them, is still valuable because it is an insurance policy. When we buy car insurance, we do not hope to be able to make any money from it; if we do, we are likely to be worse off than if we did not. But we buy "peace of mind." The same may be the case here.

The second possibility is that there are transfers received mostly by the middle class that our concept of disposable income fails to catch. This is particularly true for the European welfare states with socialized health systems and public education. Benefits that are derived from both are not included in disposable income. (Disposable income is just the cash income that is ours to spend or save; if we receive free medical care or free education, these benefits are received in kind and are not part of disposable income.) Yet free health care and education are being paid out of people's direct taxes. It is likely that while we estimate middle-class taxes correctly, we underestimate middle-class benefits because some are received in kind. Thus, were we somehow to account for the cash value of these benefits, it might turn out that the middle class does reap a net benefit from government redistributive policies.

Both of these explanations are possible, but, unfortunately, we lack the data to clearly prove either of them. But we are left with one additional interesting question. Let us go back to the very poorest, who, as we have seen, are the biggest beneficiaries of government redistribution. Suppose now that the situation of this poorest group becomes even more dire: Their market income share, already very exiguous, diminishes even further. What will happen? Will the redistribution process kick in for the drop in the share or not? It turns out that the answer is an unambiguous yes. In advanced democracies the decline in the market-income share of the poorest will be compensated, one for one, by more redistributive government tax-and-transfer policies. This is, overall, a comforting message, particularly at a time of crisis. If people who are at the bottom of the income ladder, since they cannot sell their labor or have to sell it very cheaply and also lack any assets, lose even more, the tax-and-transfer system will fully compensate for this fresh shortfall.

Thus, we see that despite the large increases in disposable-income inequality in the past twenty-five to thirty years in developed countries, and despite the differences in national tax-and-transfer systems, these systems can be shown to operate probably in the way they were intended: to help the most those who start from the lowest position and to reduce the income share of the richest. What remains somewhat puzzling is why the middle class—the class that plays a pivotal role in deciding the degree of redistribution—cannot be shown to clearly benefit from such systems. This result might also show the limits of economic analysis since our voting behavior is influenced, at times even more strongly, by ideology, principles, or values. We do not live by bread alone.

Can Several Countries
Exist in One?

Much ink has been spilled in explaining the sudden collapse of the communist-ruled ethnic federations of the Soviet Union, Yugoslavia, and Czechoslovakia. Ethnic, historical, political, religious, and purely contextual explanations have all been offered. Little noticed was the following fact, valid with respect to both the USSR and Yugoslavia (although not Czechoslovakia): Both countries were extremely heterogeneous in terms of the income levels of their constituent states (called "republics" under communism). Thus, within each country, we really dealt with several countries and several levels of developments. Moreover, the income cleavages coincided with ethnic, and at times religious, cleavages. The underlying cause of the breakup has to be sought in this overlap of income and religion or income and ethnicity.

When we speak of regional income differences in the USSR and Yugoslavia, we need to explain that it does not contradict Vignette 1.5, where I argued that the overall income inequality under communism was low. The former refers to differences in mean incomes between the constituent republics, the latter to low differences in interpersonal incomes.

It is striking that such overall low interpersonal inequality coexisted with large differences in mean incomes between the republics. This implies that within each republic interpersonal income inequality must have been extremely small. Why? Because total inequality between individuals in a country, call it A, can be decomposed into two parts: (B) interregional inequality, that is, inequality due to the differences in mean regional incomes, and (C) interpersonal inequality within each region (see Essay I). Thus, if A in the Soviet Union was relatively small and B relatively high, then C must have been really, really small.

The Soviet Union consisted of fifteen republics. At the time of the breakup, in 1991, the gap, measured by GDP per capita, between the richest republic (Russia) and the poorest (Tajikistan) was about 6 to 1. We shall see (in Vignette 3.3) that in the United States, the gap between the richest and the poorest states is only 1.5 to 1. Let's look at a few other examples. In Italy, where regional inequalities are notoriously great, the gap between the richest region (Valle d'Aosta in the north, on the border with Switzerland) and the poorest (Calabria, in the southeast) is 3 to 1. In Spain, a country not exempt from regional tensions, the gap between the richest region (Madrid) and the poorest (Extramadura) is 1.7 to 1. In France the gap is 1.6 to 1 (Île-de-France region around Paris versus Nord-Pas-de-Calais), in Germany 1.4 to 1 (Berlin versus Thuringia in the former East Germany). Thus, the Soviet Union was much more regionally unequal than any of those countries.

The three Baltic republics and Russia had incomes significantly above the USSR-wide average. All other republics (eleven) were poorer than the average.[1] Nor did the gap decrease as time went by. Although creating a consistent data series for the Soviet republics is fraught with all kinds of difficulties, and one needs to hedge the conclusions with many caveats, using the first available data from 1958, we find that the gap between Russia (the richest republic then, too) and the poorest central Asian republics was only 4 to 1. Thus, the interrepublican gap was not only large but in all likelihood also increasing throughout most of the post–World War II period.

At the time of the breakup, the Soviet Union can be viewed as a conglomerate that, within its confines, held countries with income levels as vastly different as South Korea and the Ivory Coast. Can such an entity exist without massive redistribution in favor of the poorer units in order to cement national unity? Hardly. But is that extent of redistribution feasible? Would not such transfers eventually come to be resented by the richer members who pay for them? This was precisely what happened in Russia, then still part of the Soviet Union, when Boris Yeltsin was elected to the highest republican office. He gave voice to those who opposed further subsidization. Russia thus, in a way, became, together with the Baltics, the most secessionist of all Soviet republics. The rich republics just wanted out. The poor had no choice but to acquiesce.

Even more dramatic was the example of the former Yugoslavia, not only because of the way that it imploded, but because interrepublican income differences were even greater and much more striking since the territory involved was only a tiny fraction of the Soviet Union's size. One could perhaps understand that huge differences in income levels could exist in a territory of the Soviet Union, the largest country in the world whose size was two and a half times greater than that of the United States. But for Yugoslavia, a country the size of Michigan, to contain within itself republics whose income range was 8 to 1 was quite extraordinary.[2] No other country in Europe had such a level of interregional inequality. At the most developed end of Yugoslavia (the

Northwest) was Slovenia, which at the time of the breakup in 1991 had a per capita income level equal to that of Spain. At the other end of the spectrum (the Southeast) was the province of Kosovo, whose per capita income was equal to that of Honduras. So, within a country the size of Michigan, the central government had to keep happy people with the wealth of Spain and people with the wealth of Honduras. It was an impossible task. And in Yugoslavia, despite the existence of some modest redistribution through federally funded agencies, the gaps between the republics kept increasing. In 1952, when the first data for the postwar communist Yugoslavia are available, Slovenia was only four times as rich (in GDP per capita terms) as Kosovo. Forty years later, as we have seen, the gap had doubled.

A lesson from the collapse of the communist federations is that an important part of the reason for the breakup lies in the inability of communist authorities—despite their successful policy to contain and reduce interpersonal inequality—to reduce huge, historically inherited income differences among the constituent members. Going back to the question posed in the title of the vignette, this problem will continue to plague many other countries. Will China, with its massively increasing regional differences—booming coastal regions versus a much poorer interior—remain a united country (see the next vignette)? Can the European Union continue to absorb ever-poorer members without jeopardizing its own unity and viability (see Vignette 3.3)? How will Nigeria reconcile the distribution of oil revenues between its ethnically and religiously distinct states whose per capita income differences are almost 4 to 1?

Will China Survive in 2048?

In 1970, at the peak of Soviet military and political power, Soviet dissident Andrei Amalrik published a samizdat called *Will the Soviet Union Survive in 1984?*[1] The question was not only provocative but seemed downright crazy: There was a regime commanding thousands of missiles, with clear and effective lines of communication and control, an ideological appeal far beyond its borders, and a 20 million–strong single party filled with committed loyalists or pragmatists who saw in the party their way to social advancement and were thus vested in the regime. It was a system that was projecting its ideological and military power across the globe, claimed to have eradicated abject poverty and unemployment nationally, and created a new nonethnically denominated "Soviet man." But Amalrik was proven right. And his guess as to the date of the ultimate breakup was pretty close. The Soviet Union was officially dissolved on December 25, 1991.

Amalrik's title was an obvious *hommage* to Orwell's *1984*. Whereas Orwell, at the peak of Stalinization, foresaw or rather dreaded the imposition of a worldwide communist dystopia, Amalrik, at the peak of a softer version of communist rule, foresaw its demise. So the title of this vignette is, in turn, an *hommage* to the daring with which a solitary, isolated dissident in the early 1970s posed a then unthinkable question.

The single most serious threat to Chinese unity is increasing inequality. Not only has Chinese inequality almost doubled, as the Gini coefficient increased from less than 30 in the early 1980s at the start of the reforms to 45 in 2005, but the problem with the Chinese inequality lies also in its composition. To simplify matters, we can have two types of inequalities (see Vignette 3.3): The "American" type is a high inequality where rich and poor people are more or less equally dispersed across the country and there is no geographical concentration of either poor or rich people in particular states. Obviously, rich and poor do live in separate neighborhoods, but there is no "income segregation" at the level of first-tier administrative units (that is, states). Essentially, there are "only" poor and rich people, but no poor and rich *states*. The enlarged European Union's inequality is of a different type, where the main cause of inequality lies in large differences in mean incomes among the member states, and thus the poor and rich are geographically concentrated. The Chinese developments since the early 1990s, when the focus of growth shifted toward urban areas, have increasingly produced the second kind of inequality of poor and rich provinces, which is much more politically destabilizing (see the previous vignette).

Chinese growth is strongly concentrated in coastal provinces. There are five of them. They are also the richest five of China's thirty-four administrative regions,[2] not counting the three cities (Shanghai, Beijing, and Tianjin, whose GDPs per capita are the highest). These five richest and fast-growing provinces, which lie in a contiguous belt going from the North to the South (see the map on page 81), are Shandong, whose GDP per capita, relative to the rest of China, increased from a ratio of around 1 in 1990 (meaning that it was about equal to the China-wide average) to

1.3 in 2006; Jiangsu, from 1.3 to 1.6; Zhejiang, from 1.3 to almost 1.8; Fujian, from 1 to 1.2; and the southernmost, Guangdong, from 1.5 to 1.6. These five provinces have, over the past fifteen years, each gained about 20 percent on the China-wide average. Their total population (as of 2006–2007) is about 340 million, which represents about a quarter of the total Chinese population. Yet they are responsible for more than 40 percent of the Chinese gross domestic product.[3]

If we add to them the four rich city-provinces of Beijing, Tianjin, Shanghai, and Chongqing, we obtain that their share exceeds 50 percent of Chinese total output.[4] It is easy to regard the special administrative zones of Hong Kong and Macao as a natural and, of course, even more extreme, extension of the same phenomenon, and thus this "gang" of 5+6 provinces and cities, geographically continuous, trade oriented, and increasingly more affluent than the inland part of China, begins to represent a group apart.

At the other end of the spectrum, the three poorest provinces (Guizhou, Gansu, and Yunnan) have all slipped, in relative position, since the 1990s. The GDP per capita of the latter two was at 70 percent of the China-wide average; it is now only 50 percent. The poorest province, Guizhou, went from being half as rich as the China average to only a third. As we would expect, a faster than average growth among the rich provinces and a slower than average growth among the poorest provinces have dramatically increased the top-to-bottom ratio. In 1990, at the beginning of large industrial reforms, the ratio was 7 to 1; by 2006 it had risen to 10 to 1. And this does not take into account the income of probably the poorest province of all, Tibet (Chinese statistics do not publish it), which of course would make the top-to-bottom gap even greater.

INCOME LEVELS

GDP PER CAPITA OF CHINESE PROVINCES, 2006

KEY | LEVEL OF GDP PER CAPITA

- ■ Rich: 130% or More of China-Wide Average
- ■ Average: Between 70% and 130% of China-Wide Average
- ■ Poor: Less than 70% of China-Wide Average
- □ Missing or Irrelevant Data

Source: Chinese Statistical Yearbook

This top-to-bottom ratio of at least 10 to 1 is significantly greater than the same ratio that existed at the end of the Soviet Union (6 to 1; see the previous vignette). But of course things are not the same in other respects. The Soviet Union was officially an ethnic federation, so onto the economic cleavages were superimposed cleavages of ethnicity, language, and often religion. Chinese Han do represent what may be called a single people, even if their languages are different. They also have a longer history of living under a single government than, for example, was the case for the Balts and Russians, or Tajiks and Russians.[5] The economic-cum-ethnic cleavages do, however, exist in China too, at least in respect to five autonomous regions (Guangxi, Inner Mongolia, Ningxia, Xinjiang, and Tibet), where the non-Han population represents a significant minority or even a majority. All five autonomous regions fall among the poorest provinces. Han China itself does have a history of internal breakups, most famously during the period of the warring states (between the fifth and third centuries BCE), then in the third century of the modern era (the Three Kingdoms), and more recently in the 1930s as Japan created its client state in the North of China while the rest of China was split into several warring governments, Mao Zedong's communists and Chiang Kai-shek's nationalists being the most prominent ones. Even today, two Chinas, each claiming sovereignty over the other, do exist.

Thus, the dangers, lurking beneath the gradual estrangement in economic terms as well as in the outlook on the rest of the world, between the prosperous "gang of eleven" maritime provinces and cities and the rest of China cannot be minimized, overlooked, and ignored. If there is ever a danger to Chinese national unity, it is very likely to come from the economic split within the nation.

Two Students of Inequality:
Vilfredo Pareto and Simon Kuznets

It may surprise the reader that there are few theories or theoretical insights into the formation and evolution in time of income distribution among individuals.[1] This is even odder when we know that one of the pioneers of modern economics, David Ricardo, in his enormously influential *Principles of Political Economy* published in 1817, placed distribution at the center stage of economics.

How did this happen? There may be at least two reasons. First, the distribution with which Ricardo was concerned was the so-called functional distribution of income, that is, how national income was divided into the incomes of large classes: profits for capitalists, rents for landlords, wages for workers. What we are interested in here is the interpersonal distribution of income: how national income is divided among individuals regardless of whether their main source of income is from property or labor. Now, so long as all (or most) property holders were rich, and all (or most) laborers were poor, the functional and interpersonal distributions looked rather the same. You knew that if a larger share of the pie were to accrue to capitalists, total inequality among persons was very likely to go up. And the reverse was true with wages. So the concerns with the functional distribution

THE HAVES AND THE HAVE-NOTS

of income eclipsed the concern with the interpersonal distribution of income. Or putting it perhaps more accurately, the latter was subsumed into the former.

As things began to change, and a middle class whose main income source was labor began to appear, the identity between functional and personal income distributions could no longer be maintained. Economists had to develop some understanding about how incomes are distributed among citizens in societies, not only what percentage of the total income is appropriated by capitalists or workers. This is where our first hero, Vilfredo Pareto, comes in.

But before we move to him, it is worth mentioning the second reason (not often explicitly stated), why studies of interpersonal inequality are not too popular. It is a rather simple even if often wisely ignored reason. Inequality studies are not particularly appreciated by the rich. I was once told by the head of a prestigious think tank in Washington, DC, that the think tank's board was very unlikely to fund any work that had *income* or *wealth inequality* in its title. Yes, they would finance anything to do with poverty alleviation, but inequality was an altogether different matter. Why? Because "my" concern with the poverty of some people actually projects me in a very nice, warm glow: I am ready to use my money to help them. Charity is a good thing; a lot of egos are boosted by it and many ethical points earned even when only tiny amounts are given to the poor. But inequality is different: Every mention of it raises in fact the issue of the appropriateness or legitimacy of my income. Perhaps my charity will not be seen so very favorably if somebody argues that my income was acquired unjustly or illegally. Thus, it's better to pass inequality in silence.[2] Similarly, the World Bank refused to call its flagship report on the topic a report on inequality: It was, more tamely, called a report on "equity" instead. The contrast between an apparent concern about poverty and lack of concern about inequality was nicely summarized recently by English historian David Kynaston: "Everyone is happy talking about eliminating poverty, because this looks like an admirable and ethical response to the problem of inequality, while leaving the structures of power untouched."[3]

This reluctance to deal with inequality is not confined to capitalist societies. When I began to become interested in income inequality, I lived and worked in a socialist society. Inequality was then euphemistically called a "sensitive" topic, for only superficially different, but fundamentally the same, reasons as under capitalism. Every empirical study of income distribution in socialism would show that there were income differences. It was an uncomfortable thought for the rulers of the countries that had built their ideological appeal around the idea of having ushered in the era of classless and equal society. It was safer to believe that than to investigate it too closely.

Let us now go back to Vilfredo Pareto. Pareto was a strange character. Born as a marquis in Paris, in the year of the Pan-European revolution (1848), to an Italian father and a French mother, he was raised in a liberal environment of the second half of the nineteenth century, fully fluent in Italian and French, writing and teaching in both languages (he replaced Léon Walras, one of the creators of modern marginalist economics, in his chair of political economy at the University of Lausanne), yet of aristocratic frame of mind and strongly antisocialist.[4] He was, and remains, a controversial writer. As Raymond Aron writes, Pareto to some extent produces malaise in both lecturers and students.[5] His disdain for the populace was such that he undertook to explain how all religious and ethical beliefs are fundamentally nonlogical sentiments outside the logico-experimental method that characterizes science, but all of them had to be preserved and taught in order to give the population something to believe, for otherwise people would just go back to the state of nature. After stating boldly, "I am simply investigating the uniformity of the phenomena" and "not seeking to convince anyone," he, perhaps uniquely in the history of social sciences, warded off potential readers by warning them that "those who have another objective will have no trouble finding an infinity of works which will give them complete satisfaction; they need not read this one."[6] The malaise, Aron explained, stems from Pareto's attitude, which in essence says that everything professors teach is false. But the professors, Pareto argued, must persevere in this falsehood because that's the only thing the populace would ever understand, since to teach the truth would be fatal to any social order. In Pareto's jargon: social equilibrium requires belief in nonlogical sentiments.[7]

This is how Joseph Schumpeter in his monumental *History of Economic Analysis* described Pareto:

He was a man of strong passions, passions of the kind that effectively preclude a man from seeing more than one side of a political issue, or for that matter, of a civilization. This disposition was reinforced rather than mitigated by his classic education that made the ancient world as familiar to him as were his own Italy and France—the rest of the world just [barely] existed for him.[8]

Pareto wrote two influential (text)books of economics and is today, in the economics profession, remembered essentially for two contributions: Pareto improvement (or Pareto optimum) and Pareto's "law" of income distribution. The first term is used by economists almost daily; it has become part of the indispensable economic tool kit. It simply indicates that a certain change will be socially acceptable only if the welfare of each person is thereby either improved or left as it was. Basically, somebody has to gain and nobody must lose. Finding economic policies (changes) of this kind is all but impossible because almost invariably somebody loses. Thus, the Pareto improvement requirement is a tough one; it is in reality a plea for the status quo (see Essay I).

Pareto's "law" of income distribution was generated from empirical observations. Pareto, who studied to become an engineer, and whose mathematical skills were considerable, noticed the following statistical regularity. Take income level Y and ask how many people have incomes greater than Y. Let that number be N. Then increase the threshold of income level Y by (say) 10 percent. How many people will have an income higher than Y plus 10 percent? Obviously, fewer than N. Pareto thought that he discovered a regularity, a law. Whenever the threshold would increase by 10 percent, the number of people would be reduced by between 14 and 15 percent. Hence, the Pareto constant (the "guillotine") of 1.4 to 1.5.[9] He used tax data from some dozen European countries and cities around the turn of the twentieth century, and, indeed, the Pareto constant does a reasonably good job on that sample.

Ideologically, the finding greatly comforted Pareto. He argued in his sociological papers that societies are characterized by the circulation of the elites. In a probably willful and oblique challenge to Marx, who famously stated in *The Communist Manifesto* that "the history of all hitherto existing society is the history of class struggles," Pareto claimed that the "history of human societies . . . is the history of a succession of aristocracies."[10] Unlike Marx, of course, he thought that it has to continue being so. Any attempt at socialist "leveling," a big political issue of the times, is vain. What will really happen is that a few bureaucrats or workers' leaders will replace capitalists. This would be a new elite, but an elite nevertheless. There would not be any more equality than under the previous regime. And here the empirics seemed to bear him right: Whatever country or city he chose, the distribution of income looked alike, and an almost same percentage of people were to be "guillotined" as one ascended the income distribution ladder. Pareto thought that an "iron law" of income distribution was uncovered—thus spoke Pareto.[11]

Simon Kuznets, the second apostle of income distribution studies, was an entirely different man. Born in the Russian Empire (in what is today Belarus) in 1901, he was a refugee from communist Russia, emigrated to the United States in 1922, and then studied and taught at different North American universities, including, in the latter period of his life, at Harvard. He was one of the founders of the National Bureau of Economic Research, which in the early 1940s was overwhelmingly concerned with economic cycles. Kuznets' work was heavily empirical, sifting through rather scant evidence existing at the time, displaying the data in different formats, analyzing them. He is one of the few economists whose writings are (relatively) fun to read, interesting, and often (despite the passage of time) full of insights. Yet he is also an infuriatingly difficult author to cite: His sentence structure, full of caveats, subordinate clauses, and ellipses, renders him quasi impossible to be cited or easily summarized. When one needs a short, incisive statement, he needs to cut two-thirds of what Kuznets wrote in the same sentence.

Where Pareto wrote in trenchant affirmative sentences, at times intentionally provocative and outrageous, Kuznets is cautious to a fault; where Pareto claimed to have discovered laws based on a handful of data points, Kuznets treated every number with skepticism; one reveled in his aristocratic academic maverick status, while the other was a prototypical professor.

From such scant "matériel," Simon Kuznets produced in 1955 what became, and still remains, the workhorse of the modern theory of income distribution. It is a hypothesis that at the early stages of development when societies are mostly agricultural, inequality is low (as most farmers live at or close to the subsistence level). Then, as industry develops and people begin to migrate to cities, inequality increases, both because productivity and incomes in the nonagricultural sector are higher and because in cities themselves there is more income differentiation (more professions, a greater variety of skills). Finally, as societies develop further, their increased wealth allows a more broadly based educational system to emerge, reducing the educational premium enjoyed by the few who previously had higher education. The increased wealth also permits some redistribution between the classes: introduction of social security, unemployment benefits, and the like. In a nutshell, Kuznets argued, society's inequality, as it develops, charts a huge inverted U curve: From equal it becomes unequal and then returns toward equality.

This was very different from Pareto's iron law of income distribution. In Pareto's view, development or no development, socialism or capitalism, nothing changes. There is just a different elite, but the shape of the distribution is the same. In Kuznets' view, different stages of development are associated with different levels of inequality.

Whose theory was vindicated? A little bit of Pareto's and a little bit more of Kuznets'. What is considered valid from Pareto's approach is that top incomes do indeed follow something similar to Pareto's "law." The number may not be always 1.4 or 1.5, but the "guillotine" of incomes is pretty sharp and it works. This is true only for top incomes however (the richest 1 or at most 2 percent of income recipients); for all others, Pareto's law simply does not exist. And, of course, inequality differs among countries and social systems, and it also changes over time. There is no immobility of distribution as Pareto believed.

How about Kuznets' inverted U-shaped curve? Hundreds of papers have been written on it. It is in almost equal measure supported and rejected. When, at a point in time, we plot countries' Gini coefficients against countries' income levels, we find something that looks like an inverted U shape, but, it is true, only when we work very, very hard on finding it—because the first impression is one of a shapeless scatter plot. Yet it has been argued that even this vaguely looking inverted U shape is a data artifact due to Latin American countries that are at middling income levels and very unequal for reasons that have more to do with their colonial heritage than with Kuznets' theory. They alone "create" the impression of a hump. But Kuznets' hypothesis, it was said, should be studied as it was originally defined, on individual countries over time: Did they behave as predicted or not? Until recently, however, we lacked long-term data that could have enabled us to study Kuznets' hypothesis in such a way. Now, when we have the data for a number of countries, the evidence is mixed. During the Industrial Revolution, inequality in West European countries and the United States did behave as Kuznets thought it "should": There was an upswing in inequality, reaching its peak around 1860 in England and around 1920 in the United States, and then inequality started to decline.[12] So far, so good. But more recently, in the past twenty-five years, we have witnessed a sharp reversal of that equalizing tendency. Not only in the United States and the United Kingdom, but almost everywhere: Income distribution has become more unequal in China, Russia, and India. The latter three could be explained away by arguing that they are still at the middle (developing) stage. But this explanation does not work for West European countries and the United States. There, the declining portion of the inverted U curve was transformed since the Thatcher-Reagan era into a rising portion. Thus, we now have something that looks like a re-clined letter *S*, a shape like this: ∿

But we do not have any single clear theory why the evolution of inequality should be like that: up, then down, then up again . . . Is another decline to follow? *Qui sait?* It is nevertheless true that, paraphrasing Dostoyevsky's famous statement that all of nineteenth-century Russian literature had come out of Gogol's *Overcoat*, almost all that inequality economists do today has come out of Kuznets' paper written fifty-five years ago.

CHAPTER 2

ESSAY II

Unequal Nations

Inequality Among Countries in the World

When we speak of unequal nations in the world, we speak of inequality between their average incomes or GDPs per person.[1] Although such inequalities have always been present—the Roman Empire was richer, in per capita terms, than the Goths who brought it down—the differences between nations were rather small compared to what they are today. It could hardly be otherwise because most nations before the nineteenth century were barely at the subsistence level. The large differences in mean incomes between countries are the product of the Industrial Revolution, which was akin to a Big Bang that pushed some countries forward onto the path to higher incomes while others stayed at the point where they had been for millennia. Real concern with intercountry inequality—or perhaps the realization that it is an important topic—begins only then. After the Industrial Revolution, when the differences in mean incomes became apparent, intercountry inequality rose more or less continuously until the 1950s. During some unusual periods, differences between countries did not rise—for example, between the two world wars (see Vignette 2.7)—but these were the exceptions.

Differences in income among countries come in two flavors: We can calculate inequality assuming that each country counts the same, or we can give each country a weight proportional to its population. One or the other calculation produced more or less the same results until very recently, when they started to diverge. For the past thirty years or so, we have to carefully distinguish between the two.

Two additional points deserve our attention before we engage further. First is the issue of the increase in the number of nations. If there are more countries in the world—however we measure income differences between them—the overall inequality will appear larger. (If you slice one big country into smaller and smaller units, you are likely to uncover some income differences hidden in the aggregate averages, as some slices will tend to be rich and others poor.) This is indeed a real problem when we compare the present with, say, the early nineteenth century, when both the number of countries in the world was less and the data on them were sparser. The number of countries with GDP per capita data in the set of historical statistics put together and created by one of the top economic historians of the twentieth century, Angus Maddison (which will be our key source for comparing countries over time), increases from around 50 in 1820, when the first complete data are given, to 160 at the turn of the twenty-first century. But as long as we have China, India, and the countries of the rich world in the sample, we can be rather confident that most of mankind and most of the global income are included in the comparisons, even if the number of countries may be limited. After the decolonization of the world around 1960, which saw a one-off increase in the number of countries for which we have GDP data, the problem of changing the number of countries disappears because even when the countries do break up (like the Soviet Union), we can adjust the statistics so that for the earlier years we use the GDP per capita of the newly independent countries (e.g., Ukraine, Russia) rather than of countries that existed then (USSR). Thus, we manage to measure disparity in mean country incomes across a more or less unchanging number of units.

The second problem involves how we can express GDP per capita in units that are comparable between countries and across time. Without satisfying that requirement, we would be obviously entirely in the dark: How could we compare China's per capita income in 1850 with that of France in 2000? We do it thanks to a complicated project of international price comparisons that started in the 1960s. At that time, the project was limited to rich countries but has now spread to the entire world. In those massive comparison projects (the most recent one having been completed in 2005; it is the largest worldwide economic project ever undertaken), specialists from national statistical offices collect and write down local prices for more than 1,000 goods and services. Using a very complex system of mutually consistent baskets of goods among different countries, they ultimately come up with an estimate of price levels in different countries. The process essentially pins an economic number on something that is known to every tourist who has traveled internationally. For example, we know that food prices and restaurants tend to be cheap in poor countries; a very good meal in Alexandria, Egypt, will cost less than a third of what an equivalent meal will cost in Alexandria, Virginia. Many other things, from taxi rides to valet services to manicures and haircuts, are cheaper in poor countries, too. We also know that when we travel to countries like Norway and Japan, prices seem very high.

This is basically what the process comes up with: It puts an overall number on each country's price level. The U.S. price level is taken as unity, and other countries' price levels are measured against it. In the latest round of this exercise, the price level in China is 42 percent of the U.S. price level, in India 33 percent, in Brazil 58 percent, in Norway 137 percent, and so on. This means roughly that what costs one dollar in the U.S. costs 42 cents in China, 33 cents in India, 58 cents in Brazil, and one dollar 37 cents in Norway. Very clearly, the price level increases with the average income of the country, although there are some exceptions—for instance, in island nations, where transportation costs are high, price levels are generally higher than in other countries with the same level of income. Japan, despite a smaller per capita income than the United States, has a higher price level.

This international comparison process enables us to convert GDP per capita of, say, China into units that make it comparable with GDPs of other countries and years. We thus get comparability both in space (between countries) and in time (for the same country, or between two different countries, at two different points in history).

Consider China and the United States. If China's price level is 42 percent of the American price level, then to compare the welfare of people in China and the United States, we have to acknowledge that with $100 a person in China will have more than double the purchasing power of a person with the same $100 in the United States. Therefore, to compare accurately the value of goods and services produced and consumed in China with that in the United States, we have to "blow up" Chinese incomes by a factor of almost two and a half (100/42). This is the same thing as saying that to each haircut in China, to each meal eaten in a cafeteria in Hunan, we attach not their actual prices but international prices—thereby valuing each haircut in China the same as a similar haircut in the United States. The end product is that the Chinese and American GDPs per capita will now be expressed neither in yuan nor in U.S. dollars, but in what is called PPP (purchasing power parity) dollars, an imaginary currency that in principle has the same purchasing power in China and the United States. The same calculation is, of course, performed for each and every other country that participates in the International Comparison Project: When we say $PPP 1, we mean that a unit of such imaginary currency can buy the same basket of goods in India as in China as in France, Argentina, or Zambia.

We shall use these PPP dollars a lot because they represent the only way we can compare the real income of nations. And once we have GDP per capita in PPP dollars "fixed" for a given year, we can then use countries' GDP growth rates to "project" backward their GDPs per capita in PPP terms. This adds the second necessary dimension: comparisons over time.

Here's a small example that shows how this is done. Suppose that our 2005 comparison exercise tells us that the real U.S. per capita income is $PPP 40,000, and China's income is $PPP 4,000 (approximately the actual numbers). To find out GDPs per capita levels in 2004, we take the American and Chinese per capita growth rates for 2005—2 percent and 8 percent, respectively—and for the United States divide $40,000 by 1.02 (and get $PPP 39,216), for China divide $PPP 4,000 by 1.08 (and get $PPP 3,704). We can perform the same calculation for all previous years; the "older" the growth rates we have, the further back into the past we shall be able to push this comparison. By this means, we are ultimately able to answer the question that we asked in the beginning: How do we know the relationship between China's income in 1850 and France's income in 2000—or two or more countries from any point in time for which we have the necessary data?

Now that we know how we compare countries' incomes, we can go back to some illustrative calculations—just to give a flavor of the differences among countries' GDPs per capita that existed in the early nineteenth century (when our data start) and now. For example, around 1820, Great Britain and the Netherlands, the richest countries in the world, were only three times richer than India and China, the two most populous and among the poorest countries in the world. Today, the ratio between the richest and the poorest has increased to more than one hundred to one. Even the ratio between Great Britain (which is no longer the richest country in the world) and China (despite its spectacular economic growth during the past thirty years) is now six to one, double what it was two centuries ago.

We can use many other similar comparisons and measures: They will all give the same result. Intercountry income differences have become significantly greater than they used to be. This is why the Big Bang analogy is a good one: At first countries' incomes were all bunched together, but with the Industrial Revolution the differences exploded, and the countries have "flown" further apart from each other. This is called "income divergence."

Since the late 1970s and early 1980s, we must distinguish between the two flavors of intercountry income differences. If each country counts the same, the process continues as before. Income divergence even accelerated as rich countries notched up quite respectable rates of per capita growth, while middle-income countries of Latin America and Eastern Europe went into either stagnation (named a "lost decade" in Latin America) or, even worse, economic collapse that occurred at the end of communism in Eastern Europe and the countries of the former USSR. Moreover, already by far the poorest continent—Africa, unsurprisingly—experienced a calamitous period when income declined even further, approaching subsistence level in several countries (Congo, Ethiopia, and Sudan). These changes—the poorer the country, the worse its performance during the last two decades of the twentieth century—explain continued worldwide income divergence.

But the situation is very different when we look at population-weighted intercountry income differences. In this case, countries with large populations matter more than those with small ones. Two countries in particular, both poor and the most populous in the world, will matter a lot, much more than dozens of smaller countries. They are India and China—both of which registered phenomenal growth rates. Since these countries started as very poor, their high growth was globally equalizing: A lot of their citizens were brought closer to the income levels enjoyed by Europeans and Americans. This is a development of momentous importance. Moreover, the recent acceleration of growth in India has meant that the world now has two strong "engines" (China and India) of downward pressure on population-weighted intercountry inequality.

We should keep in mind several important points as we read the vignettes that deal with intercountry inequalities: that such inequalities today are much greater than they were in the nineteenth and most of the twentieth centuries (see Vignette 2.1); and that the world is an extremely unequal place where by far the largest chunk of inequalities between individuals is explained by their citizenship, precisely because the mean incomes of the countries are so different (Vignettes 2.2 and 2.3). But we have also to keep in mind two contradictory developments that occurred over the past thirty years. First, most concerning, is the continued increase in intercountry inequality when we just look at countries without being concerned with their population sizes. These large differences in incomes are one of the main forces behind migratory pressures and the desire of people from poor countries to migrate into the rich ones (Vignettes 2.4–2.6). Second, very encouraging, is the ability of China and India to begin to bridge the gap that separates them from the rich world. Since they are so populous, their economic success means a lot for global equality.

But we should also let the data speak for themselves and not get overly carried away with the undeniable success of the China-India couplet. While extraordinary success it is, the gaps between them and the rich world are still huge, and in some ways even increasing. Let us look at the positive side first. It has been thirty years since China embarked on its extraordinary journey of economic progress. Never in the history of the world have the incomes of so many people risen by so much over such a prolonged period of time. Just to get an idea of what was accomplished, consider the following calculation: Let us define one additional unit of human welfare (a "util") as the real incomes of 100 million people doubling. This is something huge: To notch up one util, the United States will have to make sure that one-third of its population doubles its income. How many such utils has China "produced" over the past thirty years? With an average population of more than 1 billion, and with a GDP per capita that rose twelvefold, it has "produced" thirty-eight utils. The United States, whose real GDP per capita increased by a factor of three since 1950, and which had an average population of 220 million between then and now, "produced" fewer than four such utils. Japan, between 1945 and today, produced eighteen. Thus, in terms of improving the welfare of mankind, the Chinese success is just "out of the ballpark"—almost ten times more impressive than the American. This is the positive part.

Now, let's put this in the context where we look at absolute income levels. In the year 2007, India's GDP per capita was $PPP 2,600, China's $PPP 5,050, and the United States' $PPP 43,200. The absolute differences are enormous. So it should be no surprise, despite their countries' fast growth, that we shall find a very small percentage of Indians and Chinese whose incomes compare with the real incomes of middle-class Americans or West Europeans (Vignette 2.2). Just a single glance at these absolute differences should suffice to put to rest all the talk about the "global middle class" (Vignette 3.2).

Here's another startling fact that flows from these differences: If the U.S. GDP per capita grows by 1 percent, India's will need to grow by 17 percent, an almost impossible rate, and China's by 8.6 percent, just to keep absolute income differences from rising. As the saying goes, you have to run very, very fast just to stay in the same place. It is therefore not surprising that despite China's (and India's) remarkable success, the absolute income differences between the rich and poor countries have widened. In 1980 the U.S. per capita income was $PPP 25,500, China's $PPP 525. Thus, the absolute difference was about $PPP 25,000 per person; today, the absolute difference is $PPP 37,000. Since these absolute differences in real income also reflect differences in productivity, we can say that the absolute gap in productivity between the United States and China (again, despite China's phenomenal success) has significantly *widened*.[2] And of course so has the absolute gap in welfare between an average American and an average Chinese. Therefore, when

Chinese leaders insist that China is still a poor country, they might do so for political reasons, but their claim also makes a lot of sense.

This divergence of incomes among countries is important for several reasons, including migration, global inequality, and the fate of cultural diversity, most of which we shall treat in the next two chapters. But it is also important for one reason with which we shall not be directly concerned in the rest of the book—namely, how it has led to a change in the way economists think about what makes countries grow rich.

According to an earlier (called neoclassical) economic theory, globalization—even if it does not involve significant movement of people but only of capital, goods, and technology as the current Globalization 2.0 does—should be accompanied by convergence in countries' incomes because poor countries are supposed, under such conditions, to grow faster than the rich. Why? First, because under globalization they should be the main recipients of direct foreign investment from the rich world. Low wages and high return on capital should attract capitalists from the rich countries to invest there. That should increase poor countries' growth rate. Second, poor countries can access the technology, already developed in the rich world, at a relatively low cost, use reverse engineering when needed, and start the process of technological catch-up. In contrast, rich countries can advance technologically only to the extent that they break new technological barriers. It is easier to copy what was already produced than to invent something new. This is another reason poor countries' growth rate should be higher than that of rich countries. Third, specialization in the production of goods where poor countries hold comparative advantage should also accelerate their growth rate. Instead of wasting their resources in building factories that will churn out goods at uncompetitive prices, poor countries should be better off, according to the theory, focusing on things that they can do well and import other things from elsewhere. Thus, a more open trade environment should help them specialize in producing really useful things. Fourth, poor countries, thanks to the free circulation of ideas, are also able to "borrow" from the rich countries' institutions and policies that have shown themselves superior in generating wealth. None of these four things would be as easily available to them without globalization.

This is how things were supposed to happen. But they did not. On the contrary, countries' incomes have, as we just saw, diverged during the current globalization, creating a quandary for economists. It's easy enough to test economics claims against the facts. Did capital flow from rich to poor countries? Not really. Capital mostly flowed from rich to rich. In the year 2007 new direct foreign investment in the United States amounted to more than $240 billion; in China (despite all the media attention it gets) new direct foreign investments were $138 billion. Direct foreign investments in China are about the same as foreign investments in the Netherlands and less than foreign investments going to France or Great Britain. But China is an exception among poor countries. Others get far less. Consider foreign investments in India: In 2007, which was the best year ever for foreign investment flows to India, they were $23 billion, one-half of the direct foreign investments into Austria. Before the exceptional 2007, India was attracting about $4–6 billion per year, about as much as what the United States gets in a week. Thus, on average, direct foreign investments amounted, in the period of their greatest expansion, 2000–2007, to only about $20 per person in Africa, $6 in India, $45 in China, and about $800 per person in rich countries.[3] Of the total amount of direct foreign investments in the period 2000–2007 (almost $9 trillion), no less than three-quarters went to the rich nations.[4] This is the reverse of what we would have expected to see. The tendency of capital to go from one rich country to another, and more recently even to flow "upward" from poor to rich countries, as rich people from poor countries, fearful for their money and lives, invest abroad, has been termed the "Lucas paradox."[5]

The Lucas paradox is unique to the current globalization. Things were very different during the British-led Globalization 1.0, conventionally dated from 1870 to 1914, when the global economy behaved more in accordance with the theory: Capital then indeed flowed from rich countries to poor ones. Just before World War I, in the period 1910–1913, almost two-thirds of all direct foreign investment flows went into the third world countries.[6] Another way to look at it is this: At the end of the twentieth century, only 5 percent of the entire transnational stock of capital was invested in countries whose income level was one-fifth or less of the U.S. level, that is, in poor countries. In 1913 that proportion was 25 percent.[7]

Technology transfers also present a conundrum. Earlier economic theory of growth treated technology as a good that is available to everybody, such that one person's use does not reduce the amount that exists for another person (e.g., my watching a television program or using software is not going to reduce your ability to watch the same show or use the same software). That meant that poor countries could easily, and for free, get the latest technology, just if they decided to do so. But according to the new way of looking at economic growth, technology is "excludable." That is, you can require people to pay for using your technology; you can "exclude" them—technology does not come free. Microsoft and pharmaceutical companies charge poor countries for their software and drug-producing licenses, although the marginal cost of production of a new software or a drug is minimal.[8]

If that's the case, then we cannot any longer hold that during globalization poor countries will have an edge compared to the rich. On the contrary, now the rich hold all the aces up their sleeve. This is why the issue of intellectual property rights has acquired such a huge importance today: Rich countries want to make sure they get money for their inventions. Poor countries see it as just another obstacle to their development. To appreciate the irony of it, note that Disney Productions loudly demands protection against the "piracy" of their DVDs, while some of their most successful films are based on stories created precisely in the countries about whose "piracy" Disney complains. But the intellectual property rights for *One Thousand and One Nights* have long since expired (or rather never existed), while Disney's rights are very much alive.

Thus, on both accounts of capital flows and access to technology, Globalization 2.0 appears to be less favorable to the poor countries than economists originally thought. If so, we can begin to make more sense out of income divergence.

Economists have introduced additional elements to explain the divergence. Perhaps, they argue, combining highly skilled people and highly sophisticated capital—both of which are plentiful in rich countries—helps increase output more than in the proportion in which capital and labor are added.[9] That too would help rich countries more than the poor: Rich countries would experience what is called increasing returns to scale (two workers plus two computers produce more than twice as much as one worker and one computer), while poor countries, at a lower technological rung, would experience the usual constant returns to scale (two workers and two textile machines produce exactly twice as much as one worker and one textile machine).

More attention is also paid to the production of new technology and new ideas. Rather than leaving the emergence of new technology largely outside of economics in a kind of caricatural "Newton principle" of technological development (an apple falls on a very, very smart guy who is taking a nap), economists now regard technology as "embedded" in a given institutional and cultural setup and subject to incentives. It has thus become "endogenized" into a given economic system, rather than left outside economics strictly speaking (as something that just happens—or does not happen). The implication of this new view is that rich countries that have developed institutions conducive to research and development of new technologies will produce a disproportionate number of inventions. These inventions and innovations are in turn viewed as key for spurring economic growth—yet another way in which the finding of income divergence between rich and poor countries can be explained.

Empirical facts of income divergence during the past thirty years have thus led to (1) a closer look at the empirics of economic growth, capital flows, and access to technology that were found at odds with what economists expected before Globalization 2.0 set in; and (2) a revision of the economic theory of growth, which now includes a different view of technology transfers, a new perspective that regards technological progress as "endogenous," namely, produced by specific institutions and cultures, and a more important role for increasing returns to scale. The uncomfortable facts of Globalization 2.0 have led to a reassessment of theory and an attempt—we still do not know how successful—to revise it to fit these facts better.

Vignette 2.1

Why Was Marx Led Astray?

One of the recurrent themes in Marx's writings from *The Communist Manifesto* to *Das Kapital* is the increasing polarization of society into workers and capitalists. As was customary at the time, workers were assumed to live at, or close to, subsistence, while property owners gradually amassed greater and greater fortunes. This ever-increasing polarization should, according to Marx, eventually produce a proletarian revolution.

It was not an entirely wrong depiction of reality at the time. Great Britain, a prototypical capitalist society from which Marx drew most of his conclusions, underwent during the entire eighteenth century and probably the first half of the nineteenth century a steady and sustained rise in inequality.[1] Other developed capitalist countries like the Netherlands and Germany also experienced increasing inequality.[2] Moreover, inequality was sharply polarizing: on the one hand, poor and numerous workers; on the other hand, richer and ever-fewer capitalists.

Combining (a) high inequality within advanced capitalist nations and about equally high inequality elsewhere (India, China, Russia, Latin America) with (b) relatively small differences in GDP per capita among the countries (for example, in 1820 GDP per capita of the Netherlands, the richest country in the world, was only three times greater than GDP per capita of China, one of the poorest countries of the world)[3] gives us (c) a picture of global inequality where within-national income differences are in the driver's seat. If we call these within-national differences "class" differences (our point *a* above), and the between-national differences in mean income (our point *b* above) "locational" differences, we find that, for explanation of global inequality in the nineteenth century, class has been much more important than location. So far this fits the Marxist scheme of things beautifully: With escalating class differences within nations, and relatively little difference in the average living standard among nations, the seeds are sown for a revolution both nationally and worldwide.

But in an ironic twist of fate, it is precisely around the publication of the first volume of *Das Kapital* in 1867 (the only one published during Marx's lifetime) that things started to change. A new data series of English real wages produced by Gregory Clark shows that it is around 1867–1870 that real wages began their secular rise that continues (with some small declines from time to time) to this moment.[4] Moreover, it is around the end of the nineteenth and in the first half of the twentieth centuries that income differences between the rich world of West Europe, North America, and Oceania, and the rest of the world (Africa, Asia, and Latin America) exploded. This was indeed the period that saw the birth of what we today call "the third world."

Thus, the Marxist picture that only a couple of decades earlier seemed reasonable came to be profoundly altered by around 1900. The world was no longer divided into proletarians who were everywhere equally poor and capitalists who were also, everywhere across the world, equally rich. On the contrary, workers of the developed capitalist countries started becoming richer. The gap between them and their less fortunate colleagues in poorer countries, whether muzhiks in Russia or coolies in India, began to grow. The solidarity that was assumed to exist between the proletarians around the world and was emblazoned on the International's flag in the famous dictum "Proletarians of all countries, unite!" began to fray and eventually evaporated.

In the second half of the nineteenth century and with increasing frequency toward the end of the life of Marx's coauthor, Friedrich Engels (he died in 1895), the concept of a "workers' aristocracy" came into existence. Engels himself mentions it several times.[5] Workers in developed capitalist countries realized that they had more to lose than their chains, as Marx claimed in *The Communist Manifesto*. When Trotsky upbraided German Social Democrats, the most powerful left-wing party up to 1914, often regarded as the certified guardian of Marx's teachings, he contemptuously wrote that the German party would not lead the workers' revolution because it was loath to ruin impeccably laid-out German lawns.[6]

From the left-wing perspective, the world, at first slowly, and then more quickly, changed. The proletariat, the class that could bring the world revolution along, was no longer present in all nations. It was harder and harder to find common points of interest between the relatively rich workers of West Europe and North America and the workers who slaved away in countries colonized by the bourgeoisie of the rich countries (the bourgeoisie, which, however, shared some of the spoils with its domestic working class, thus estranging workers from one another). The discourse of revolution changed, and this change was eventually best reflected in Mao Zedong's claim that the third world was the new proletariat, while the classes to be overthrown were

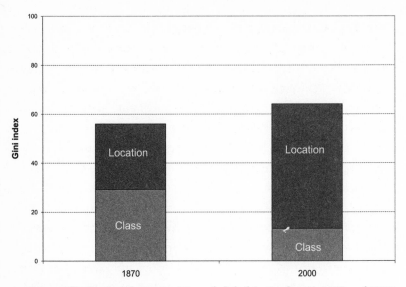

FIGURE 2 The level and composition of global inequality in 1870 and 2000 (Gini decomposition)

Note: The height of the bar indicates the level of global inequality.

Sources: François Bourguignon and Christian Morrisson, "The Size Distribution of Income Among World Citizens, 1820–1990," *American Economic Review* (September 2002): 727–744; Branko Milanovic, *Worlds Apart: Measuring International and Global Inequality* (Princeton: Princeton University Press, 2005), fig. 11.3.

those from the rich countries, combining implicitly in the latter group pell-mell workers and capitalists of the first world. The ideas of both the universal proletarian brotherhood and the "permanent revolution" were given up.[7]

Marx's world had thus gone topsy-turvy in some 150 years. Why? Because the underlying global income distribution had changed. Around 1870 global inequality between world citizens was less than it is today (see Figure 2). But the most striking thing is not its overall magnitude but how its composition changed: From being predominantly driven by class, it has changed to being almost entirely driven by location (80 percent of global inequality). Today, it is much more important, globally speaking, whether you are lucky enough to be born in a rich country than whether the income class to which you belong in a rich country is high, medium, or low.

The divergence of incomes between the countries has drawn the spear through the heart of Marx and his followers' vision of solidarity among the exploited classes. But could there perhaps be some solidarity among the poor nations of the world? After decolonization in the 1960s, and then during Mao's rule in China, growth of the nonalignment movement, and the quest for the New International Economic Order in the 1970s, that seemed to be a possibility. Yet that solidarity in turn was undermined by several key developments over the past twenty-five years: the phenomenal growth rates of China and India and the steady "embourgeoisement" of several formerly third world countries like Taiwan, South Korea, Malaysia, and Chile. Today, South Korea and Chile (and increasingly China and India) have much more in common with France and the United States than with Angola and Cambodia. Moreover, a third world "solidarity" would have probably come to take markedly nationalistic overtones, as were, for example, present in Japan's ideology of a "coprosperity sphere," which it foisted on its hapless Asian neighbors during World War II. But nationalisms tend to cancel each other out; no true solidarity can be built on the backs of several nationalisms. In conclusion, neither global class nor cross-national solidarities seem possible today because the underlying material conditions of people are simply too different. Friends and foes are too heterogeneous to be defined by any binary scheme, least of all by a binary scheme based on income alone.[8]

The fact that most of global inequality is presently due to the differences in mean incomes among countries, that is, what we called "location," has its own important implications. After reviewing inequality today more fully in the next vignette, we turn to two such implications: What does it imply for our incentive to work hard and improve our own lot, and what are the implications for migration?

How Unequal Is Today's World?

We are used to thinking of countries, and thus of people, as averages. Almost every day, we hear or speak of the GDP per capita of such and such country. Being so used to it, we have almost forgotten the meaning of it. GDP per capita is an *average* measure: It sums up the value of all goods and services produced in a given country (or area) and divides it by the number of people who live there. It is not necessarily an actual income of anyone; it is just an arithmetic average.

To get a real picture of the world of incomes, we need to break down the country averages (like GDP per capita) into actual incomes received by people in each country. This "true" picture of the world is, as we shall see, both more reassuring and more alarming than the usual per capita picture. It is more reassuring because we shall find that there are people who live in poorer countries and who are richer than some people who live in richer countries (which of course is excluded by looking at the averages only). But it is also more alarming because we shall find that in many cases practically *all* people living in a richer country are better off than *all* people living in a poorer country.

A proper picture of world distribution thus has to combine these two aspects of within-national and international distributions. This is shown in Figure 3. Consider how it is created. Take the United States, which is here used as a representative of the rich

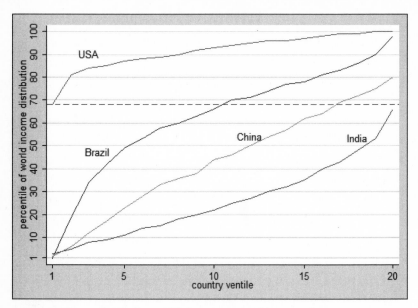

FIGURE 3 Inequality in the world, by country and income class

Note: The graph shows that the income of the poorest 5 percent of Americans (country ventile 1 on the horizontal axis) situates them at the 68th percentile of world income distribution (see the horizontal broken line at level 68). The interpretation for all other points is the same.

world, though any other similarly rich country would do. We take the entire population of the United States and divide it into twenty income groups ranked by their household per capita income from the poorest to the richest. Each group is called a ventile (from *venti*, like in Starbucks coffee shops), indicating that there are twenty such groups. Each contains 5 percent of the American population. We do the same "slicing" of all countries in the world. Each ventile will therefore "enter" with its own average income expressed in local currency. This income is converted into international (PPP) dollars of equal purchasing power so that in principle, with such a dollar, a person can buy the same amount of goods and services in India as in the United States or anywhere else in the world. This enables us to compare incomes worldwide.

Once the national ventile distributions are created and their PPP dollar incomes calculated, we find the position of each ventile in the global income distribution. Again consider the United States. Since the United States is a rich country, most of its population will be highly placed in the world income distribution. The poorest American ventile, as shown in the figure, is at the 68th percentile of the world income distribution (see the horizontal line at Y=68). This means that the poorest Americans are better off than more than two-thirds of the world population. People in all other (higher) U.S. ventiles are, of course, even better off, and the richest Americans belong to the top world percentile. The same interpretation holds for other countries.

Now, the United States is not only a rich country on average (and hence its ventiles highly placed), but a country of moderate inequality compared to other countries shown here (although not compared to West European countries). The span between the richest and the poorest ventile in the United States is 32 global percentiles (100 − 68). But in China, the distribution covers a much wider range, from the 3rd to the 85th percentile. Brazil, with its unequal income distribution, covers practically the entire global spectrum, going from the lowest percentile to the richest. It can thus be seen as a microcosm of the world, since a world distribution will be a 45-degree line rising steadily from the 1st to the 100th percentile. Brazil contains in its midst some of the poorest and richest people in the world. We can see now why the use of country averages is misleading. For example, about one-half of the Brazilian population is better off than the poorest American ventile.

India, in contrast, is fairly poor, with its poorest ventile belonging to the 4th-poorest percentile in the world and the richest ventile only to the 68th. This last value shows that the richest people in India (as a group—admittedly a large one since it contains more than 50 million people) have the same per capita income as the poorest people (as a group) in the United States. This latter fact is striking—and alarming. There are many countries in the world whose top income classes are poorer than the poorest income classes in rich countries. For sure, if we were to break national distributions into smaller units, not in ventiles of 5 percent each, but in percentiles (1 percent each), we would find some overlap. But the overlap is still tiny. In the case of India and the United States, only about 3 percent of the Indian population have incomes higher than the bottom (the very poorest) U.S. percentile.

We could continue for a long time with similar examples. Instead of India and the United States, we could use Cameroon and Germany (only 5 percent of Cameroonians have a higher income than the poorest Germans), the Ivory Coast and France (12 percent overlap), Zimbabwe and Great Britain (8 percent overlap), Congo and Belgium (5 percent overlap), and so on. In many cases the overlap is minimal: Citizenship is fate in the sense that it guarantees a person either a high or a low income. This has, as we shall discuss in the next three vignettes, huge economic implications. But let us here focus on just one implication of a situation where the income overlap between the rich and poor countries' populations is minimal. Suppose that we have to decide whether the United States should give aid to a country that looks like Brazil or to a country that looks like India, and we do not know how such aid will be used or who would be the beneficiaries in either country. The argument in favor of giving aid to India will not be based solely on the fact that its average income is lower. It will be based also, and perhaps more importantly, on a very low probability that such aid would entail a "regressive" transfer, that is, a transfer that would flow from a relatively poor American taxpayer to a richer Indian recipient of aid. With countries such as India, regressive transfers are practically ruled out. If the average U.S. taxpayer's income is located around the 90th percentile of the world, there are almost no people (in any statistically significant numbers) around or above that income level in India. But the situation is different in Brazil: Some 5 percent of the Brazilian population have incomes that are higher than the income of our notional U.S. taxpayer. In consequence, regressive income transfers between the United States and Brazil are more likely than between the United States and India.

The "true" picture of income distribution in the world should also help us deal with "everyday" problems like the allocation of aid given by rich countries. Not unlike in the domestic policy arena, where it is not appreciated that unemployment benefits financed by taxpayers be received by people who are richer than the taxpayers, in the international arena too, we should strive to minimize the likelihood of such "regressive" transfers. This means taking into account not only the mean incomes of the countries but their income distributions as well.

How Much of Your Income Is Determined at Birth?

We have already seen not only that the world is a very unequal place, but that it is also unequal in a very particular way, that today most of its inequality stems from very different average incomes among countries. One's income thus crucially depends on citizenship, which in turn means (in a world of rather low international migration) place of birth. All people born in rich countries thus receive a location premium or a location rent; all those born in poor countries get a location penalty.

It is easy to see that in such a world, most of one's lifetime income will be determined at birth. More exactly, in a regression where we have the actual incomes of everybody in the world (of course only in principle, because the data are based on national income surveys, which are only samples of national populations), plotted against their countries' mean incomes, it turns out that place of birth explains more than 60 percent of variability in global incomes. In addition, each 10 percent increase in average income (GDP per capita) of one's country of birth raises a person's income by the same 10 percent, so that within-national inequalities are shown to play only a small role in global income distribution (because the same countrywide tide carries more or less everybody from that country equally). It is that *levels* of income in different countries are vastly different, and they are the main factor that explains global inequality.

But we can go one step further and try to determine how much it is worth being born not only in a rich country but also to rich parents. We use the data on each country's intergenerational income mobility (that is, the correlation between parents' and children's incomes) and probabilistically determine in what income classes were parents of children whom we currently observe in a given income class of the United States, or Canada, or Morocco. To see how this is done, suppose that a country has very little intergenerational mobility (say, as in Pakistan). In that case, people whom we currently observe in Pakistan's top income class will have almost entirely come from parents who themselves belonged to high income classes. The opposite is true when there is high social mobility: Then people whom we currently observe in top (or bottom) income classes will have come from parents randomly distributed along income distribution. In real life, countries will cover a vast spectrum between these two extreme positions.

Using this information, in addition to the place of birth (or, more exactly, citizenship), allows us to explain a person's income in the world by only two factors, both of which are given at birth: his citizenship and the income class of his parents. These two factors explain more than 80 percent of a person's income. The remaining 20 percent or less is therefore due to other factors over which individuals have no control (gender, age, race, luck) and to the factors over which they do have control (effort or hard work).

Explaining away one's income thus shows that the portion left for effort must be very, very small. Yes, one can try hard to improve one's position in a given country (provided that the country has a tolerable income mobility between the generations), but these efforts may often have a minuscule effect on one's global income position.

We can understand this point by using the following metaphor. Imagine global income distribution as a long pole on which income levels are marked from the bottom, around the subsistence minimum, to the maximum household per capita income in the world. Imagine then each country's distribution to be given by a plaque, running along the pole, and covering the range of that country's income distribution: India's plaque, for example, will run between relatively low values, Korea's between middle and top values, while that of the United States will tend to cover high values. When a person is born, he gets pinned down to a place on his country's plaque that not only gives his position in national income distribution but also locates him in global income distribution.

How can he improve his position? His own effort or luck may push him up the national plaque if his society "accepts" some income mobility. But this cannot, from a global perspective, play a large role because more than 80 percent of variability in income globally is due to circumstances given at birth. So that route can, at most, yield very modest results. He can hope that his country will do well: The country's plaque will then move up along the global pole, carrying as it were the entire population with it. If he is lucky enough that his own effort (movement higher up along the plaque) is combined with an upward movement of the plaque itself (increase in the national mean income), he may perhaps substantially climb up in the global income distribution. This is the experience of many young Chinese today.

Or—a last possibility—he might try to "jump ship," that is, move from a lower plaque (poorer country) to a higher one (richer country). Even if he does not end up at the high end of the new country's income distribution, he might still gain substantially. Thus, one's own efforts, one's country doing well, and migration are three ways in which people can improve their global income position.

The role a person's effort plays is small; he cannot influence his country's growth rate, so the only alternative that remains is migration. That's the topic to which we move next.

Should the Whole World Be Composed of Gated Communities?

In an unequal world where income differences between countries are large, and information about these income differences is widespread, migration is not a fluke, accident, anomaly, or curiosity. It is simply a rational response to the large differences in the standard of living.

The amount of migration flows is tiny compared to what it would be in a world of free migration of labor. Currently, the flow of people from poor countries to rich countries (the latter conventionally defined as Organization for Economic Cooperation and Development [OECD] countries) is about one-twentieth of 1 percent of the poor world's population annually. Roughly speaking, that means that it would take two centuries for 10 percent of the poor world's population to relocate to the rich world.[1]

The migratory pressure is much greater than these numbers suggest. Where is it the strongest? Clearly, migration responds to many elements like cultural affinity (the same language or a shared history), accidents of previous migration, and so forth, but the two elements with which we are concerned here are large differences in the average standard of living and geographical proximity. When they are present, we should expect a large migratory pressure even if other factors (like common language) are absent. If we look at the map of the world, we can identify four such "pressure points": North Africa and Spain (divided, at the narrowest point, by 13 kilometers of the Mediterranean Sea); Mexico and the United States (sharing a common land border); Albania and Macedonia, and Greece and Italy (sharing a land border, or being, in the case of Albania and Italy, separated by about 85 kilometers of the Ionian Sea); and Indonesia and Malaysia (separated by as little as 2.8 kilometers in the Strait of Malacca). What is remarkable in these four cases is that only in the last one do people speak the same language (Malay and Indonesian versions of Bahasa). In the three other cases, languages are different, and so are the dominant religions. Thus, it is not cultural but rather purely economic factors that are behind migrations.

The gap in average incomes between the emigrant and immigrant countries is in all four cases in excess of 3 to 1 (after adjusting for the lower price level in poor countries and thus reducing the gap compared to what it would have been with currencies converted at the market exchange rate). This means that people from the poor countries can, by what we called "jumping ship" in the previous vignette, improve their standard of living approximately threefold. The gap is not only huge but increasing. In 1960 Mexico's GDP per capita (in PPP terms) stood at 1 to 2.5 against that of the United States; in 2005 the gap rose to 1 to 3.6. In the 1960s Spain was about four times as rich as Morocco; today, it is seven times as rich. Figure 4 shows GDP per capita of a poorer country expressed as a percentage of GDP per capita of the (relevant) richer country. Notice the general downward trend in the past quarter century. It should not be surprising that migration pressures are building.

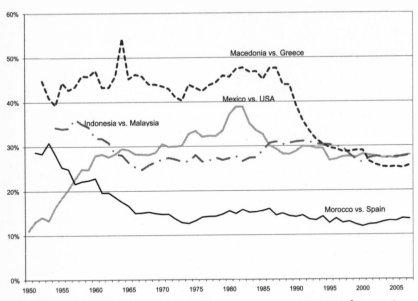

FIGURE 4 Per capita income of emitting country as a percentage of per capita income of the recipient country, 1950–2007

And indeed, when we consider the five recipient countries, the share of foreign labor in each of them is high. The foreign-born labor force, including undocumented aliens, is estimated at 15 percent in the United States, around 17 percent in Spain, at least 14 percent in Malaysia, 9 percent in Greece, and 7.5 percent in Italy.[2] As we would expect, the largest foreign contingent in the United States is (by far) Mexican; in Spain, it is Moroccan; in Greece, Albanian; and in Malaysia, Indonesian.

In a recent World Bank study, people from seven countries were asked whether they would move to another country (permanently, temporarily, or "just to try it out") if it were legally possible.[3] A whopping 62 percent of Albanians expressed interest in moving permanently or temporarily out of their country; for Romanians, the percentages were 79 percent for males and 69 percent for females; for Bangladeshi, 73 percent for males and 47 percent for females. In this small sample, we see that countries that have done economically poorly would, if free migration were allowed, remain perhaps without half or more of their populations. With fully open borders, we would witness enormous migration flows that would almost empty out some parts of the globe. There is little doubt that a large share of the African population, particularly the youth, would inundate West Europe, the part of the world that is colloquially known in some Congolese languages as "the heaven."

But migration is a two-way affair. It is not only that poor people want to move to rich countries; there must be enough jobs that wait for them there. And indeed, the movement of labor is possible because there is a pull (demand) element too, although often in the informal or undocumented sector. But while the pull element exists from specific enterprises or sectors, the inflow of immigrants creates a generalized backlash, because it is perceived to (or effectively does) crowd out jobs for the locals, reduce their wages, and, most important, introduce different cultural norms.

The issue of migrant assimilation does not have the same urgency everywhere. Countries that are themselves created by immigrants, like the United States or Canada, are thought more resilient and able to absorb the newcomers. Countries of Europe, for a long time the main emigrant countries themselves, have many more problems dealing with the cultural distinctiveness brought on by immigrants. This is true even when those "culturally different" are their own citizens, born in West European countries. Yet they are not fully accepted. Thus, second- or third-generation German-born Turks until recently did not qualify for German citizenship that was based on the blood line (*ius sanguinis*). Among the French, there is a not-too-subtle distinction between the *Français de souche* (those with French roots) and others. Until widespread riots in the summer of 2005, led mostly by disaffected North African youth, the French government did not even acknowledge the problem. Legally, everybody was the same: French. It did not matter, in the eyes of the government elite, that black or North African French could not make it to top schools or were hardly represented at all among the most lucrative professions. There was not a single black French announcer on the state television network.

Whether it is under the pressure of domestic labor or out of fear of cultural heterogeneity, the rich world has begun a process of walling itself in, creating de facto gated communities at the world level. The most infamous of them is the U.S.-Mexican border fence that is supposed to run for seven hundred miles. It is, at times, a twenty-foot cement wall, reinforced by barbed-wire obstacles and equipped with numerous cameras and sensors. The Mexican Wall should, when fully constructed, be seven times as long as the Berlin Wall and twice as high. Nevertheless, it is estimated that more than 200,000 Mexicans enter the United States illegally every year,[4] and that at least 400–500 die trying to cross the border.[5]

The European Union cannot erect a fence across the Mediterranean but is using hundreds of speedboats to interdict access to its shores by desperate Africans and Maghrebis. A couple hundred thousand are estimated to risk their lives annually, taking rickety boats mostly overnight to avoid detection. Several hundred are thought to perish.[6] A conspiracy of silence from both sides envelops the dead. The Europeans are skittish to reveal the extent of this human catastrophe lest it undermine their self-image of "protectors of human rights." The African countries either are indifferent to the fate of their citizens or treat illegal emigration as a crime (e.g., in Tunisia it is punishable by three to twenty years of jail and a fine). Even the families of the dead are not too keen to publicize their fate. Thus, these unknown and ignored people die daily, their bodies decomposing in the cold waters of the Mediterranean or scorching heat of New Mexico, and nobody has an interest in mentioning them, counting them, or even acknowledging that they existed and died.

One such group is known as "the burners of papers," the Maghrebi *harraga*. Who are they?

Who Are the *Harraga*?

They are called the "burners of papers," although they could also be called "the burners of borders." They burn their own papers so that when they make it to Europe and the governments there try to send them back to their countries, the police are confused: They do not know if a *harga* (singular of *harraga*) is from Algeria or Morocco or Tunisia. Keep the enemy confused!

The *harraga* are almost entirely young men, between twenty and thirty-five years old, from the Maghreb. But to understand the problems faced between the Maghreb and the soft Mediterranean underbelly of Europe, one has to speak of three actors in this unfortunate drama. Starting from the south, the first actors are poor sub-Saharan Africans who desperately try to reach the heaven of Europe. They do it either directly, by boats from the western coasts of Africa to the Canary Islands (the nearest European-controlled land in Africa), or more frequently by going to North Africa, that is, to Libya, Morocco, Algeria, or Tunisia, and trying to get to Europe from there. In that perilous journey, many die. Frantz Fanon's *les damnés de la terre* have been transformed into *les damnés de la mer*.

The second actors in the drama are the Maghreb's own emigrants, the *harraga*. They are physically closer to Europe and can cross the Mediterranean directly. Yet there are differences in the distance to, and accessibility of, Europe from different points of the southern shore of what in an oblique reference to the cold war they call "the Mediterranean wall." Many of the *harraga* thus congregate in the areas of northern Libya or Tunisia. The most well-known ports of departure, out of which, mostly at night, they board the small boats overloaded with human cargo, with no lights and with only very primitive navigation equipment, are Zuwarah and Tripoli. Both are in Libya. Libya has become a key transit nation, not only for Africans, who are estimated to number more than 1 million (accounting thus for one-sixth of the Libyan population), but also for fellow Arabs. They stay illegally in Libya, working as construction workers, fishermen, or repairmen; are treated brutally;[1] and bide their time—either trying to save some 1,000–1,500 euros that a human trafficker charges per person (half of that amount for children) or waiting for the opportune moment, a propitious dark night, a good wind, to embark on one of those fragile boats.

The third actor in the drama is Europe, the target of these expeditions. As the inflow of immigrants has increased, Europe has been shutting its doors more and more tightly. Fast boats, almost military in their looks, equipped with infrared-vision cameras, airplanes, and electronic fences are used to spot and send back the emigrants before they can reach a European shore. The EU operation of interdiction called Frontex costs 40 million euros annually. Ironically, this is about the same amount as the "transport fees" paid by some 40,000 African emigrants who arrived by sea in Italy in 2008 alone, an increase of 75 percent compared to the year before.[2] After interdiction, the next part of the European strategy of "deterrence" is to sign bilateral agreements with the riparian countries that oblige the latter to receive back their migrants, to conduct joint patrols of the seas, and in the case of Libya (which is the most cooperative among African nations) even to open refugee camps for the prospective migrants on their own territory. It is there that those who try to move to Europe remain and wait until the decisions on their asylum or expulsion are made. Thus, Europe tries ever harder to push its virtual borders farther and farther south to make sure that as few as possible potential migrants make it to European soil.

Once they do touch down on EU soil, the problems become more complex. They cannot be immediately sent back but must be "processed," resulting in a long period of waiting, during which the migrants have to be fed and sheltered, until eventually they are either granted political asylum, refugee status, or temporary permission to reside in a European country or repatriated by force back home. The question then arises: where to keep these thousands of people—the ones who have survived the voyage, made it past the European speedboats, and reached the promised land? Even there Europe tries to push its borders as far as possible from its "core." The tiny island of Lampedusa, which is closer to Tunisia than to Sicily, has been selected for this role. More than a thousand are "imprisoned" there in a camp that was originally planned to host some seven hundred. The conditions are unbearably bad. The camp that was originally called the "Center of Reception and Emergency Aid" was in January 2009 rebaptized by the Berlusconi government as the "Camp of Identification and Expulsion." The change in the name says it all. In February 2009 the refugees, despairing that the inhumane conditions in which they were being held would ever get better, rebelled. The camp exploded into riots, and a fight between the guards and would-be future citizens ensued. A part of the former "Center of Reception and Emergency Aid" was burned down.

Lampedusa is only one of those European camps. A similar camp, Hal Far, exists in Malta—a camp where African refugees had to hang a huge banner reading "We are humans!" to attract passersby's attention to the people living there cordoned off by the barbed wire.[3] In Spain, which every year expels around 100,000 illegal immigrants, the government has to deal with an even more macabre problem: what to do with the dead bodies of the *harraga* when they float to the beaches and in midsummer scare off tourists who have come to forget all their daily worries on the beaches of southern Spain? The Spanish government has recently asked the Algerian government to take more than 170 bodies that have thus far been found. But the Algerians refused: first, for not being able to identify the bodies, and, second, for not being sure that the corpses were indeed Algerian (and not Moroccan or Tunisian).[4]

But perhaps the Algerian government refused for a more profound reason: not to hear the message that the *harraga* send about the failure of North African societies to provide these young people with any hope of a normal and decent life. This is the issue, constantly swept under the carpet, not only by the Europeans but even more so by the North African governments. Until recently, almost nothing was officially said or written about these people. Even families were afraid to admit that they had *harraga* in their midst. It was a national and family shame, best ignored.

These people who try to leave their countries of birth for the uncertain pleasures of Europe are not only poor; they do not see any future, any place for themselves, in their own societies. Their desperate bids to reach Europe are silent accusations leveled against the governments that are unable to provide any social

THE HAVES AND THE HAVE-NOTS

and economic perspective to the growing multitudes of the young. They are also an indictment of the economic failure of Arab and sub-Saharan Africa, a testimony to the increasing income gap between the two shores of the Mediterranean. In reality, as Ali Bensaad, a Franco-Algerian sociologist, says, "one should salute the tenacity and courage of the harraga. Lacking any channels of political . . . expression, those are the youth who react with the elements they have constructed from a devastated cultural and political space, emptied of all meaning by their governments."[5]

Can this insoluble equation be solved? Can a globalized world, where capital, goods, ideas, and information travel without impediment, coexist with a world where humans cannot move? Can these two separate and unequal worlds coexist when income differences between countries are huge and getting ever larger? Not only are the *harraga* from all poor lands more likely to be around for a long time, but their numbers will continue to increase—and with them, the grim statistics of suffering and death.

The Three Generations of Obamas

The lives of the three generations of Obamas nicely illustrate several key themes of this book.

In Barack Hussein Obama's (BHO) beautiful little book *Dreams from My Father*, it is—however remarkable a man his father was—his Kenyan grandfather who receives the most attention and appears in the most formidable light. The grandfather, Hussein Onyango Obama, was born in 1895, left home very young, struck out on his own, despite all communal pressure to find himself a wife, demurred, and, after years of hard work, eventually received some belated and begrudging social acknowledgment thanks to his farming abilities.[1]

Onyango's life was not usual. After leaving the ancestral home, he began wearing Western dress and went looking for a job in Nairobi. The best that this hardworking, stubborn, and impressive man could find was to be a manservant to the British. Colonialism has erected a very visible, impenetrable ceiling, no matter how ambitious or smart a black person might be. Higher positions were only for the British. Onyango seems to have accepted this state of affairs: He never rebelled against it openly, he spoke against Kenyan independence, and he was deeply upset by his son's (BHO's father) marriage to a white woman. But he probably resented the uneven treatment, or at least realized the enormous injustice it involved.

THE HAVES AND THE HAVE-NOTS

In the Kenya of the 1920s and 1930s, the separation in terms of social position and income was not *nearly* complete; it was complete. As there were no higher positions available for blacks, there were no lower positions available for whites. This is what in the economics of inequality is technically called "no overlap" between the two distributions: Anyone who was white was better off than anyone who was black. (Note that in Vignette 2.2, we find a similar thing to hold in many comparisons between rich and poor nations today.)

But we can even put some numbers on this yawning gap. BHO quotes from his grandfather's work booklet called *Domestic Servant Pocket Register* that all native Kenyan workers were obliged to carry when working or looking for a job. In the booklet previous employers would write their observations, positive or negative, about the worker. One of Onyango's employers, in one of the apparently few negative comments on his work, wrote that Onyango "was found to be unsuitable and certainly not worth 60 shillings per month."[2] This remark was written in the early 1930s (the booklet was issued to Onyango in 1930). Taking Onyango's normal salary to have been (as written in the booklet) 60 shillings per month, his annual income works out to be 720 shillings.[3] Because at that time his family included a wife and a child, the annual household per capita income was therefore 240 shillings.[4]

Thanks to the studies of the economic history of Kenya, we have an estimated income distribution of Kenya for the year 1927.[5] The poorest and by far the largest social group (accounting for 82 percent of the total population) consisted of African smallholders with an estimated annual income of 137 shillings. This is the level just around the subsistence minimum. Next came African agricultural workers (7 percent) and African self-employed (1.2 percent), with estimated household per capita incomes of 211 and 271 shillings, respectively. This is where Onyango's family was situated: better off than approximately 90 percent of the population of Kenya and an even slightly higher percentage of the black Kenyan population.

Yet how far from Asians and Europeans living in Kenya! An estimated average per capita income for Asians was 3,300 shillings, some fourteen times more than that of Onyango's family. The average income of a European (who represented, according to the census, one-third of 1 percent of the population) was an almost incredible 16,000 shillings. The current U.S. president's grandfather was thus working as a manservant or cook in a household of people whose incomes were sixty-six times greater than his own. Onyango would have to work for an entire year to make as much as his British employer would make in less than a week. This was not an aberration but a typical distribution of incomes under colonialism. As will be seen in Vignette 3.7, in almost all colonies, the incomes of the vast majority of the indigenous population were barely above the subsistence level, and income differences between them were minimal. Obama's grandfather was nominally among the top 10 percent of the population according to income, but just barely better off than the subsistence farmers. At the very top, however, among the richest 1–2 percent of the population, mostly or entirely composed of colonizers, incomes would simply shoot up to almost unimaginably high levels.

As mentioned, despite the fact that *Dreams from My Father* is concerned principally with retracing BHO's father's life, we learn, in some ways, less about the father than about the grandfather.

Nevertheless, what we do learn about the father is sufficient to illustrate the new possibilities that independence opened up to Kenyans. The ceiling on native Kenyans' incomes and social position was removed: They could claim the highest-paid jobs and become bosses, high-level public servants, or rich traders. It is difficult to imagine that under colonial rule, Barack Obama Sr. would have had a chance to study in the United States. To be sure, the idea to go to the United States for study was given to him by two American women who found him very clever and diligent. And, yes, there were some Africans who acquired higher education even under colonialism. But the end of colonial rule removed both an effective and a psychological barrier to claiming higher positions in life. What could a university-educated African do with his fancy degree when the country was run by foreigners—get a job as a subaltern office worker? But in 1960 the limits were lifted.

Barack Obama Sr., having graduated from Harvard, went back to Kenya. That too illustrates the postcolonial era of optimism when the native children believed that their rightful place was back in their own country, which, thanks to the knowledge they acquired at the best schools, would be brought out of underdevelopment and into the modern world. It was certainly a much more optimistic time for young Kenyans than it is today. And this was not the case just because the oppression was lifted and the possibilities suddenly appeared almost endless, compared to how constricted they were under colonial rule. It was also because the income gap between Kenya and the developed world was much less than today.

Paradoxically, as we know, independence has not solved Africa's problems. On the contrary, during the period of independence, Africa has slipped much further behind the developed world. African countries either became even poorer than before independence or failed to advance at the same speed as the rich world. The income gap between the United States and Kenya, which was thirteen to one when Barack Hussein Obama Sr. came for schooling to the United States, had opened up to thirty to one by the time his son assumed the presidency of the United States of America.

I wonder what Barack Obama Sr. would have thought more absurd as he set out on his improbable journey to the New World in 1960: to believe that his son would become the ruler of the country that he had never laid his eyes on or to believe that his newly independent land would become twice poorer (compared to the United States) than it already was?

And what about Barack Obama Jr., the president? His life story illustrates so many things, on which so much has been written, that little new can be added. Yet, in terms of our topic, in terms of the rising "citizenship premium" that is acquired by those fortunate enough to be born in the rich world (see Vignette 2.3), perhaps it is best to let Barack Obama Jr. explain it himself. Here is why his mother decided to send him away from Indonesia when he was only eleven years old to stay with his grandparents and attend high school in Hawaii:

> She had always encouraged my rapid acculturation in Indonesia. It had made me relatively self-sufficient, undemanding on a tight budget, and extremely well mannered when compared to other Americans. She had taught me to disdain the blend of ignorance and arrogance that too often characterized Americans abroad. But she now learned . . .

the chasm that separated the life chances of an American from those of an Indonesian. She knew which side of the divide she wanted her child to be on. I was an American, she decided, and my true life lay elsewhere [outside of Indonesia].[6]

Did the World Become More Unequal During Deglobalization?

One of the truisms of simple neoclassical economics is that openness to the movement of labor, capital, and goods—that is, globalization—should not only benefit all participating countries but benefit more the poor ones.[1] This is based essentially on three assumptions. First, poor countries are "producing" a higher marginal return to each successive addition of capital than the rich countries. Since the rate of profit in poor countries will be greater than in rich countries, capital will flow to the poor world. Second, technology, which is all-important for economic development, is exchanged more easily when borders are open. The primary beneficiaries of technological transfers are also poor countries. They have to pay little or nothing in order to imitate the technology invented in the rich world. While the developed countries have to invest a lot to make technological breakthroughs and create inventions, it is relatively easy and cheap for poor countries to benefit from these inventions by copying them. They leapfrog technological developments. Nigeria does not need to spend time and effort building land phone lines, nor does it need to invent cell phone technology. It can ignore the old technology and simply imitate Nokia, setting up a cell phone factory itself. Third, and somewhat novel, is a reason that has to

THE HAVES AND THE HAVE-NOTS

do with institutions. As countries integrate, they also come to know better what type of institution works best. Suppose that we all agree that it involves strong protection of property rights and financial deregulation. Then, poor countries that generally have less "efficient" institutions will again benefit more because they will be able to imitate the better institutions of the rich world.

We have seen in Essay II that these simple predictions were found quite wrong when it came to explaining the growth of the world during Globalization 2.0. This fact is by now generally acknowledged, and alternative theories of economic growth have been proposed to account for it. It is also accepted that since the Industrial Revolution, the average incomes of the countries of the world have diverged (see Vignette 2.1). But what has happened during the period of deglobalization when, if the theory is correct, we should observe an increase in the differences between poor and rich countries?

The period of deglobalization, conventionally considered as spanning the years from the end of World War I to the beginning of World War II, is one of the least studied by economists. The problem, from the economists' point of view, is that it is a political period par excellence. The October Revolution in 1917 "subtracted" from under the capitalist control one of the key countries in the world with the largest landmass. The birth of fascism in Italy in 1922, with its many imitators in Central and Eastern Europe, further "downplayed" the role of economics because fascist states, while being capitalist (in the sense that they protected private property rights even more fiercely than the liberal regimes they overthrew), imposed a much greater role for the state in the economy and tended to see trade in mercantilist terms, that is, as a zero-sum game, not as mutually beneficial.

The chaos of the civil war in China and the brutal colonization of Africa (again, a noneconomic action) further limited the scope of "free" economics. And the final nail in the coffin was the rise of National Socialism in Germany. Thus, economists believe that the interwar period can teach us, if anything, that politics *à l'outrance* cannot be good for economic development.

And indeed, this lesson is true. But an interesting question is whether this set of negative developments had the expected effect on the growth of poor and rich countries. Of course, the world was much "smaller" then. Not only did it have fewer independent countries than today, but the data for many countries (most of them colonies) are not available. So we have to work with a sample of some forty-five countries that includes poor countries like China, Nepal, and India at the one end and rich countries like the United States, Australia, and New Zealand at the other end. Although the data for Africa are almost entirely missing, our global population coverage is around 90 percent because the African share in world population at the time was less than it is today.[2]

When we calculate a battery of inequality measures across this sample of countries, inequality shows no apparent tendency to either go up or down over the entire period, whether we begin the study in 1913 (just prior to the outbreak of World War I) or in 1919 (at its end). For example, in 1913 the ratio between the income of the richest and poorest countries (respectively, the United States and China) was just under ten to one. That ratio increased to twelve to one on the eve of the Great Depression and was about eleven to one in 1938 (with the Netherlands replacing the United States as the richest country in the world and China still being on the bottom).

We can conclude that all the many commotions and deglobalization that the world witnessed between 1913 and 1938 left the inequality among nations unchanged. As we saw above, this is not what we would expect from simple neoclassical economics. But two interesting subperiods can be highlighted. First, what was the impact of the Great Depression? And second, what was the impact of the Second World War?

We start with the latter because these results are unambiguous. The Second World War, even in this incomplete sample, clearly had a strongly disequilibrating impact. The main "beneficiaries" of the war were already the richest countries, like the United States, Switzerland, New Zealand, Australia, and Canada. Thus, between 1939 and 1945, GDP per capita of the United States increased by an extraordinary 80 percent (growing at the modern "Chinese" rate of 10 percent per annum), Canada gained almost 60 percent, Australia and Switzerland 20 percent, Argentina 10 percent, and so forth. On the other hand, Germany lost more than 20 percent of its output, the Soviet Union between 10 and 18 percent,[3] France almost 40 percent, and Greece and Japan more than one-half, while the data for the most devastated countries of Eastern Europe (Poland and Yugoslavia) are not even available. From other sources, we can estimate their losses to have been in excess of 50 percent. China too, already on the bottom in the world income league in the 1930s, slid even further in absolute amounts as onto the chaos of the civil war were superimposed the disaster of the Japanese occupation and the war of national liberation. The Second World War produced a massive divergence in incomes among the subgroup of rich Western countries, but more importantly in the world as a whole, too. It benefited the rich countries on whose territory it was not waged (note that all the "gainers" remained outside the

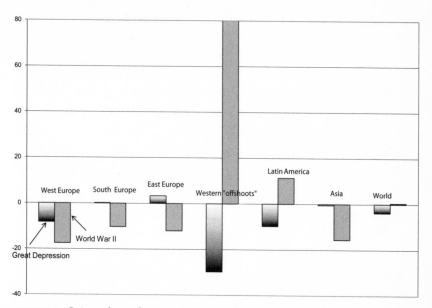

FIGURE 5 Gain or loss of per capita output between 1929 and 1933 and between 1938 and 1945 (in percentages)

Note: Regional means are population weighted. The data for the period 1929–1933 include forty-three countries with a 1933 population of 1.8 billion (around 90 percent of the total world population); for the period 1938–1945, the data include forty-three countries with a population of about 1.2 billion (60 percent of the total world population). China is not included in World War II totals. With China, total world output change would turn from slightly positive (as in Figure above) to slightly negative.

Source: Calculated from Angus Maddison, *Contours of the World Economy: Essays in Macroeconomic History, 1–2030 AD* (Oxford: Oxford University Press, 2004).

scope of military operations), and it destroyed a huge amount of physical capital among the belligerents on whose territories it was fought. In terms of regional groupings, the Western Hemisphere and Oceania gained, while everybody else lost (see Figure 5).

Now, the Great Depression had a very different overall effect. Among the rich world, the three countries that suffered the most

were Canada, the United States, and Germany. Between 1929
and 1933 the United States and Canada lost 30 percent of their
per capita income, Germany about 20 percent (although it re-
bounded in 1933 after Hitler's assumption of power). Next came
France, Spain, and the Netherlands, which lost more than 10
percent, Great Britain with a loss of some 5 percent, and so
forth. But a number of poorer countries went through the Great
Depression relatively unscathed: Japan and Korea (under Japanese occupation) continued to grow; the same is true for China
(which, as we have seen, was in the 1930s the poorest country in
the world). The Soviet Union, whose first five-year plan was
launched in 1928, grew by at least 20 percent, and so did an as-
sortment of countries such as Portugal, Norway, and Turkey. If
we look at the effects of the Great Depression by region, the
most severely affected were the "Western offshoot" countries, the
United States, Canada, Australia, and New Zealand (who were
later the main beneficiaries of World War II), and the least affected were Eastern Europe (thanks to Soviet growth), South
Europe, and Asia (see Figure 5). Overall during the Great Depression, the world lost some 4 percent of per capita income.
This is in contrast to World War II, which, in human lives, cost
in excess of 50 million, but in terms of global per capita output
might have seen at most a decline of 0.5 to 1 percentage point
(indeed only when we include the value of all airplanes, sub-
marines, ammunition, and tanks produced together with consumption goods).

CHAPTER 3

Unequal World

Inequality Among Citizens in the World

You might think that it would be easy to combine the inequality among individuals within nations and inequality between nations and estimate the extent of global inequality across all citizens of the world. This is, unfortunately, not the case.

First, we lack the necessary data. While the data on GDP per capita that go into the construction of between-country inequalities can be reasonably well estimated from the early nineteenth century (and, as we have seen, even for the ancient societies, like the Roman Empire), the data on within-national distributions are much more recent. The household surveys we need to calculate income differences among individuals within each single nation are much harder to get than just a summation of values of goods and services produced. Beyond that, to create something that approaches a global distribution, we must have household survey data for all important countries of the world (both those important in terms of population and those important in terms of total income), covering at least 90 percent of the global population and global income. This benchmark was reached only by the mid-1980s when the three large areas, from which income distribution data were not available or accessible before, joined the rest of the world: China, whose first full-fledged national household income surveys became available in the early 1980s; the Soviet Union, which conducted far from perfect, but nevertheless useful, surveys since the late 1920s but did not want to make them available before the mid-1980s and the introduction of *glasnost*; and finally, countries in Africa that for many reasons, from weak statistical agencies to lack of resources, did not field household surveys at all. That too changed around the same time with the greater involvement of international agencies, in particular the World Bank. These three serendipitous developments opened the doors for the first exact estimates of global inequality, based entirely on direct estimates of individual incomes rather than on guesses about the shapes of national income distributions.

Beyond the problems with the data, until recently income distribution was seen purely as a national issue, not a global one. There was no need to think about or compute seemingly irrelevant concepts like global inequality. It is only with the rise of globalization, with closer and more numerous contacts among peoples of different nations and continents, as well as with the timid emergence of something that may be considered "the incipient institutions of global governance," that it began to make sense to compare our incomes with the incomes of faraway peoples—not only as an average against another average but as one individual versus another. In a globalized world, the number of our peers has multiplied manifold.

A close historical parallel to this process is the simultaneous rise of the nation-state, centralized national governments, and interest in national income distributions. Prior to the rise of the nation-state, when countries consisted of often-isolated towns, villages, and hamlets whose citizens interacted only infrequently, and might have been even unaware of what new sovereign a monarchical rearrangement on the political map had brought them, there was certainly neither the need nor the ability to measure individual incomes within a country. When Pareto became interested in the empirics of national income distributions (see Essay I and Vignette 1.10), it was because public awareness of the problem already existed, and the data, however fragmentary, were available. It is similarly not entirely accidental that the data that made possible the inquiry into global income distribution appeared about the same time that task became intellectually interesting and challenging. As Marx wrote: "Mankind . . . inevitably sets itself only such tasks as it is able to solve, since closer examination will always show that the problem itself arises only when the material conditions for its solution are already present."[1] In this case, indeed, the problem of global inequality arose around the same time that the data to study it first became available.

Once the interest and data existed, it was relatively easy to collate national income distributions into one giant global distribution and calculate, for the first time ever, global inequality— treating the world as if it were a single country. A series of results have been generated for the benchmark years, at approximately five-year intervals, running from 1988 to 2005.[2]

The results show, not surprisingly, that global inequality is extremely high. Its Gini coefficient reaches the value of 70, which is higher than inequality in any single country in the world, even in such paragons of inequality like South Africa and Brazil that exhibit Ginis of "only" around 60.[3] We reach the Gini of 70 when the individual incomes of people living in poor countries are adjusted for the lower price levels they face. If we use their actual dollar incomes instead, inequality is even higher and reaches a Gini of 80. But what does a Gini of 70 (or 80) really mean? Has global inequality, at least from the time we can directly measure it, gone up or down? What can we say regarding the causality between globalization and global inequality?

Today's global distribution of income is such that the richest 10 percent of income recipients receive 56 percent of the global income, while the poorest 10 percent receive only 0.7 percent of the global income. The decile ratio—the ratio between the average income of the top 10 percent and the bottom 10 percent—is about eighty to one. For a useful comparison, within a "usual" developed country, that ratio seldom exceeds ten to one. Another way to look at the global distribution is to consider the share of the top 5 percent: 37 percent of the global income. The share of the bottom 5 percent is less than 0.2 percent of the global income. Thus, the ratio between the top and the bottom of the global pyramid reaches almost two hundred to one: To make what the richest make in a year, the poorest would have to work over an improbable two centuries. Such examples can be multiplied—and are more dramatic the higher we go up (and down) the pyramid.

The gaps are magnified when we look at them in simple dollars terms (that is, not PPP dollars that adjust for the lower price level in poor countries). Then the top 10 percent receive more than two-thirds of the total world income, while the top 5 percent get 45 percent. The shares of the bottom 5 and 10 percent of people are almost negligible.

Has the distribution become more uneven since the late 1980s? The most considerate answer to that question is probably not. The household-level data that we use to construct these distributions, of course, have their own problems—and they are many. There is what the statisticians call a large noise-to-signal ratio, that is, there are among the surveys idiosyncrasies in the data collection, differences in the definitions of income components (how best to impute the value of one's housing? how to value home-produced and -consumed goods? how to distinguish between enterprise and household incomes for many self-employed people?), and differences in the willingness of the rich to participate. Our Gini estimates thus come with rather large standard errors. Since 1988, when such global inequality calculations were first conducted, the Gini coefficient has remained at about the same level of 70; each "reading" has been within one standard error of every other.

But this is only a technical, accounting, part of the explanation. A more substantive issue is that global income distribution in the past thirty years has been determined by three forces, two of which pushed it up, and one—albeit a powerful one—that pushed it down. The forces for greater inequality were the rising income differences within most of the important (as well as smaller) nations, which we discussed in Essay I. Remember that to get to global inequality, one needs to add to intercountry inequalities those inequalities that exist within each country. Consequently, the rise in this last element will push up global inequality. The second force that pushed global inequality up was the divergence in country mean incomes, with poor countries growing more slowly than the rich, which we discussed in Essay II. But the third force influencing global income distribution was an equalizing one, namely the fast growth of China and India (also discussed in Essay II). When China and India set off on a path of fast growth, they were (and still remain) relatively poor: If poor economies grow faster than the rich, inequalities diminish.

Thus, basically, if we want to think of global inequality—a topic that can be rather difficult to grasp because we must juggle many balls at the same time—we can simplify it posing three key questions:

1. Are within-national inequalities generally rising or not?
2. Are poor or rich countries on average growing faster?
3. Are China and India growing faster than the rich world?

Since the mid-1980s the last force has roughly balanced the first two. The last force is also the most important, because intercountry differences account for the bulk of global inequality— and were one of the other two, thus far disequalizing, forces to change direction, we would probably witness a strong decline in global inequality. On the contrary, were China's and India's growth rates to sputter and fall to the level of the world average or less and the first two forces to keep going unchecked, there is little doubt that global inequality would rise again.

Globalization and global inequality. Can we establish causality between globalization and changes in global inequality? The answer is both very difficult and context specific. The channels through which globalization affects global inequality are very complex. First, globalization affects the national income distributions of poor and rich countries, and may affect them quite differently—for example, increasing inequality in rich countries and diminishing inequality in the poor. Second, it affects differently the growth rates of poor and rich countries. Third, it may affect differently the growth rates of very large, mid-sized, and small countries. Thus, just to disentangle all these effects borders on the impossible. On each of them there exists a huge scholarly literature, with empirical results that often cover the entire spectrum of the possible. No consensus exists on the effects of globalization on any of these three channels through which it influences global inequality.

But there is also a deeper reason why this question can be answered only within a specific historical context. Suppose, for the sake of the argument, that we all suddenly agree about the issues on which we just said there is a lively scholarly dispute: say that globalization does not influence at all national income distributions and makes the growth rates of poor and populous countries faster compared to the growth rates of rich countries. Wouldn't that be nice? Since one effect is neutral, and the second and the third effects are proequality, globalization must, on balance, be good for global equality. But the answer still depends on where the populous countries fall in the income distribution spectrum of all countries. If most of the populous countries are poor, as is the case today and as we implicitly tend to assume, then the previous conclusion would be valid: Globalization will be good for equality. But if we "decouple" poor and populous countries—since there is nothing fundamental that dictates that the populous countries must always be poor (after all, the United States is a very populous country, the third most populous in the world, yet one of the richest)—then the situation changes: The convergence of national mean incomes is still good for equality, the fact that national inequalities are undisturbed is neutral, but now if globalization is good for populous countries—and they are rich—then global inequality can easily go up.

This example illustrates one simple thing. Even if we agree on the role that globalization plays with respect to each channel whereby it affects global inequality, the contextual, historical shape of things (where in the income distribution of nations the populous countries are) will determine the ultimate answer. There cannot be a general answer to the question "How does globalization affect global inequality?"; there can at best be only contextual answers. And for the past thirty years, our best attempt at that contextual answer would be to say—as we already did—that its role was ambivalent: There were forces that pushed for greater inequality and others that offset it (most notably China's and India's growth).

The whales that carry the world on their back. To have a closer look at global inequality, it is not sufficient just to compare the incomes of the top and the bottom. What is important is to find out *who* is in the top and *who* is in the bottom. We have discussed earlier (see Vignettes 2.1–2.4) how large are the intercountry differences in incomes, so we are not going to be surprised to find that citizenships of people in the top and bottom parts of the global income distribution are very different. Take the top 1 percent, roughly the 60 million richest individuals in the world. Almost 50 million of them are citizens of West Europe, North America, and Oceania (see Vignette 3.1). We can next look at the top decile. The situation is not much different there. More than 70 percent of the people in the top decile are from the rich Western nations, next come Asian countries with a share of 20 percent, Latin America with less than 5 percent, and East Europe/former Soviet Union and Africa with very small shares. There are no Chinese or Indians (in any significant numbers) among the people in the top global decile. There are, though, more than 2 million South Africans and 7 million Russians. The situation among the bottom decile is of course very different. There, 70 percent of people are from Asia, about a quarter from Africa, and some 5 percent from Latin America. There are no East Europeans or citizens of the rich Western countries among the lowest global decile.

But the best, and perhaps graphically the most pleasing, way to look at this is to construct a pyramid. To do this, after ranking people from the poorest to the richest, we need to ask the following question (five times): How many poorest people (then less poor, then middle income, and so on) are needed to generate successive 20 percents of global income? Obviously, when we ask the question the first time, the number will be large. It turns out that it is 77 percent of the world population. This is the bottom of our pyramid. Next we ask, how many people are needed (now clearly somewhat better-off individuals) to generate the second 20 percent tranche of total income? We need 12 percent of the world population. And so on, until we come to the last 20 percent of the global income. For that, we need only 1.75 percent of the people in the world. The top of the pyramid, in terms of people, is small; the bottom is large. The results are shown in Figure 6. Not only is the pyramid's slope sharp, but the picture reminds us of the old idea of the world as a plate carried on the backs of several whales. The whales in this metaphor, however, are the poor people of the world.

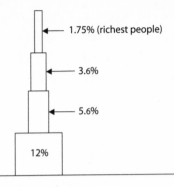

FIGURE 6 The global pyramid: What percentage of people in the world do you need to generate successive 20 percents of global income?

Note: The width of each block is proportional to the percentage of people. The height of each block is the same (since each block contributes 20 percent of the global income).

The evolution of global inequality over the long run. Although we have reasonably accurate data about global inequality for the period since household surveys for most countries in the world became available (post-1980s), it is much more difficult to establish its evolution before that time. Thanks to some recent work, the willingness to use some heroic assumptions about how national income distributions in the past might have looked,[4] and, not least important, the fact that we know that the main engine driving global inequality has resided in intercountry differences in GDPs per capita (on which we have better data), we are able to say something about global inequality in the past. François Bourguignon, one of the top economists working on income distributions, and Christian Morrisson, a French economic historian, have estimated that in 1820, global inequality was 50 Gini points; then it rose to 61 in 1910, 64 in 1950, and finally to 66 in 1992, when their study ends.[5] The shape charted by global inequality since the Industrial Revolution is one of a steady, but diminishing, increase: The curve has been rising but has, in the past twenty or so years, reached a very high plateau.

Its future direction is not easy to predict. According to a renowned American sociologist, Glenn Firebaugh, and an equally renowned economist and Nobel Prize laureate, Robert Lucas, we have been going through a gigantic "inequality transition," and the worst of inequality is behind us—or is just with us right now. In the future, global inequality will be driven down by the continued fast growth rates of China and India.[6] This is quite possible, but one has to be cautious before drawing too hastily on the inevitability of uninterrupted economic progress in these two countries. There are many unforeseeable circumstances (see Vignette 1.9, with respect to China) that can derail their progress. One needs also to realize that this prediction depends on specific movements in one or two countries, not on any general trend, where the large number of cases might ensure movement in a given direction even if individual cases have "the liberty" to move out or against this general trend.

A smooth downward slope of global inequality cannot be guaranteed even if China and India continue with their current growth rates, because in some twenty years, when they would pass the level of middle-income countries, their own growth would become globally disequalizing if other large countries like Indonesia, Bangladesh, Nigeria, and Pakistan remain far behind.[7]

Inequality among citizens of the world is today probably as high as it has ever been, although this high point stands on a plateau of very high inequality rather than alone on a peak. Global inequality has been rising, first quickly, then more slowly, but nearly uninterrupted since the Industrial Revolution. And very importantly, the composition of global inequality—the forces that make it grow—has changed over the same period: From being dominated by within-national inequalities it has become to a large extent determined by intercountry inequalities in mean incomes (see Vignette 2.1). The relative income positions of China, India, and the United States play a crucial role in determining its level and evolution.

Does global inequality matter? Jagdish Bhagwati, a Columbia University economics professor, in his book *In Defense of Globalization* termed every statistical work on global inequality—let alone concern with it!—no less than "a lunacy."[8] Others make a similar claim, even if they couch it in less incendiary terms, because there is no "addressee" to whom complaints about too high inequality can be directed. In a single country, people share the same government; if they feel that inequality is too high or society too unjust, they have a political mechanism—elections in a democracy, revolt in an autocracy—to make their concerns known. And the rulers, whether democratic or not, must, for reasons of self-preservation, take into account, in their thinking and decision making, the views of the population.

But at the global level, so long as there is no global government, dissatisfaction with the level of inequality cannot be meaningfully expressed or translated into political action, the opinions cannot be conveyed to anyone, and, most important, there is nobody who can act upon it. Thus, some argue, for inequality to be a socially relevant issue, that is, for people to be both concerned with inequality and willing to do something about it, there must be an associative relation among people that is lacking at the global level. This is called the "political conception of distributive justice." As explains one of its key proponents, Thomas Nagel, "Justice is something we owe through our shared institutions only to those with whom we stand in a strong political relation. It is . . . an associative obligation."[9] The political conception of distributive justice does not rule out humanitarian duty of assistance to foreigners, but it also does not impose on rich people and rich countries anything beyond that.

Philosopher John Rawls offered a different view of why global inequality is immaterial. Rawls saw the most desirable global arrangement as the one where conditions from his *Theory of Justice* (see Essay I) are satisfied for each individual country; at the global level different rules hold, and the duty of assistance of rich countries is limited in extent and time (see Vignette 3.8). In other words, a just world is a world populated by just states. Period. In Rawls's view, a global optimum is achieved once individual country-level optima are reached.

Instinctively, none of this feels right. The fact that the income of the top 1.75 percent of the world's population matches the income of the poorest 77 percent does not seem either good or optimum or a needless cause for concern. There are at least two good reasons it does matter. We may regard inequality instrumentally. Large income gaps between countries are driving socially unsustainable international migration flows. Locally, high inequality among communities and individuals is associated with political instability. These national political instabilities tend to spill over to neighboring countries and even to the rest of the world. For *instability* in that sentence, read *chaos*. Recent examples, as diverse as piracy near the shores of Somalia and the Mexican flu, illustrate how local poverty (which is just a different word for global inequality) easily affects the rest of the world. In one case, poverty and anarchy in Somalia threatened to bring to a standstill international shipments of oil in one of the most sensitive areas of the world; in the other case, poverty and bad sanitary conditions within Mexico led to the flu epidemic that quickly spread to the four corners of the world, infected thousands, and killed several hundred people. In other words, high levels of global inequality make global chaos more likely.

Second, we can also adduce ethical arguments for lowering global inequality. We do not need to limit the domain of our concern with justice and duty of assistance only to the people with whom we share political institutions—that is, those in the same country. These same concerns kick in as soon as what political philosopher Charles Beitz calls "consequential relations"— relations of some importance—are established between individuals regardless of where in the world they are.[10] These may be relations of trade, migration, and investment, as well as relations mediated by international organizations like the World Bank, International Monetary Fund, World Trade Organization, or climate-change bodies that impose rules of conduct and have significant effects (whether for the good or bad) on individuals from diverse countries. As soon as such rule-defining international organizations come into existence and there is a sufficient "density" of economic relations (that is, enough people interact or trade with each other or enough people are affected by the actions or rules emanating from these institutions), the duty of justice, and hence concern with global inequality and redistribution, emerges.[11]

An even stronger position is held by the so-called cosmopolitans, who regard the world as composed of persons who all have an equal moral value and an equal moral claim on each of us. In this view, neither familial relations nor geographic proximity nor shared institutions privilege one group of people over another. We should (perhaps some already do) regard all of them simply as individuals equally worthy of our attention and concern.[12] In such a case there cannot be any real distinction between inequality at the national and global scales. Both are equally important. Whatever we have said in favor of lower inequality nationally (see Essay I) must hold globally, too.

The trilemma of globalization. The trilemma of globalization, to use a phrase coined in a somewhat different context by Harvard economist Dani Rodrik, is how to continue with (1) globalization while (2) the differences in mean incomes among countries are huge, and increasing, and (3) the international mobility of labor remains very limited. These three things, which have so far characterized Globalization 2.0, cannot be endlessly maintained. Globalization naturally leads to better knowledge and awareness of living conditions across the globe, which, if income differences between countries are large, stimulate migration. But, as we have seen (Vignettes 2.4 and 2.5), large-scale migration is not politically acceptable for the rich countries, and they create ever-greater obstacles to it.

In the long run the antimigration battle cannot be won—if globalization continues. A much better alternative would be to help reduce differences in average income levels between countries. In that case, migratory pressures would subside, and the world would, from the point of view of the standard of living, become a much more homogeneous place, not threatening the continuation of globalization. Otherwise, if both large income gaps between countries persist and rich countries limit or pre-vent migration, globalization may have to be scaled back. The interdependence of these three key recent developments is not sufficiently appreciated. But the options are relatively simple—and stark: For an ever-closer integration of economies and peo-ples to proceed, either poor people's incomes have to be raised in the countries where they currently live, or they will come, in ever-greater numbers, to the rich world.

Where in the Global Income Distribution Are *YOU*?

Many people have seen or used the Internet sites that give your position in global income distribution. You may be asked to enter just one number, your income, and in no time the site tells you, hocus-pocus, your position in world income distribution. (For the sake of full disclosure, I have seen a couple of these sites that claim to use, in order to produce such distributions, the data from my book *Worlds Apart*. I was not involved with anything they did, nor do I know how their calculations are performed.) But now I propose to do something similar here.

The Internet sites' guesses are probably wrong, not necessarily because they do not have the best data (which may be true too), but because they do not take care to explain the information that needs to be inputted in order to meaningfully locate one's position in global (or, for that matter, national) income distributions.

Thus, we need first to do some homework. I may soon start sounding like the IRS, but unfortunately you will need to do three things. First, you will have to find out how many members are in your household, then calculate your total annual household income, and then decide how to deal with this most troublesome of issues, housing costs or imputation of housing benefits.

Let's start with the household size. Members of your household are people with whom you generally take meals at home and who sleep under the same roof as you. It includes long-term visiting relatives or friends but excludes domestic help or tenants (both of whom might live under the same roof as you). It excludes also children who live outside the home, even if you may pay for most of their expenses (e.g., children in college). This may seem strange and arbitrary but is not. The assumption is that household members share everything evenly. Thus, a long-term visiting relative will equally partake in food, housing amenities, and so forth, but also will have to contribute his or her income to the household. But your kids, living outside the home, are already separate household units. Even if you pay for their expenses, this is considered a voluntary private transfer. It is your decision to help them. Technically, you could have used that money to buy a new car or go on a vacation, but you get more pleasure from helping your kids.

Next we move to the IRS-like part of the homework: deciding what your household income is. You have to add wages and Social Security income (pensions) of all family members, income from various assets family members own (e.g., rental property, interest on banking accounts, profits if you have an entrepreneurial activity, returns from your stocks and bonds, and the like). Since everything will be done on an annual basis, you should look at the annual income from each of these sources. It is often very hard to define entrepreneurial or self-employment income, but we have to suppose that you can do it here no worse than when you filled out your tax form (although expenses that one may claim to the IRS to reduce one's taxable income are not generally accepted when we define household income for statistical purposes). Even capital gains should be included as part of income, so you should add them, too.[1] After that, you need to deduct direct taxes paid by all household members. For countries where taxes are deducted at the source (the same way that compulsory Social Security contributions are deducted at the source in the United States), things are simpler: One does not need to bother with deducting them. There, the take-home wages already exclude direct taxes.

Now, we come to a very tricky issue, that of housing. For many complicated reasons, we mostly shall have to ignore it, but the logic ought to be explained. Take, for example, two people with an income of one hundred dollars each, but one owns his home and the other rents it. Common sense tells us that the first must be better off. Indeed, that's why we need to add to his one hundred dollars the imputed value of the housing services he enjoys, that is, the rent that he would have paid if he were renting the house. This gets really complicated because most people's situations fall somewhere in between: They are neither 100 percent owners, nor pure renters. They might have paid off part of their mortgage (say, one-half). In that case, they should impute only one-half of the estimated rent. This is the part for which they live "for free." However, for practical matters here and because we want to have a conservative estimate of income, it would be best to skip the housing imputation altogether and not add anything to your income *unless* you own the house or apartment outright. Only in that case should you add to your income an estimated rent.

We now have to do only one more thing, which unfortunately has to be done very roughly, too. We need to adjust the income that you have calculated so far by the price level of the country where you live. We compare the welfare of various people who live in different countries, and we have to take into account the fact that price levels differ among countries and that in India you need fewer dollars to live equally well as in the United States (see Essay II). Generally speaking, the poorer (on average) the country where you live, the lower the price level and by more (upward) do you have to adjust your calculated income. If you live in the United States, there is no adjustment to be made because the international calculations are so arranged that the U.S. price level is made equal to the international price level. You can, if you wish, just multiply your calculated income by 1. As a rough rule of thumb, if you live in West Europe, Australia, or New Zealand, you should reduce the income you calculated by about 10–20 percent on account of higher prices there; if you live in "cheaper" South European countries like Turkey, Greece, or Portugal, you should increase it by 10–20 percent. If you live in East Europe (including Russia) or Latin America, multiply it by a factor of 2; if in China, Africa, or Indonesia, multiply it by a factor of 2.5. Finally, if you live in India, multiply it by 3. Only if you live in Egypt, Bolivia, or Ethiopia may you multiply it by a factor of 4.

Now, we are ready. Take the number that you have obtained from your income calculations, add the housing imputation (if any), divide by the number of household members, and adjust by the price level of the country where you live.[2] Write the final number down on a piece of paper.

If your income is greater than $PPP 1,225 you belong to the upper half of global income distribution.[3] Let us aim higher. To be in the top 40 percent, your income needs to be about $PPP 1,770 per capita; to be in the top 30 percent, you need $PPP 2,720.

After a certain level, the necessary threshold to jump a few additional percentage points ahead rises fast: To be among the top global quintile (the richest 20 percent of people in the world), you need $PPP 5,000 per year, and for the richest decile, your income ought to be at least $PPP 12,000. For the top 5 percent, the requirement is $PPP 18,500. And for the top world percentile, the threshold is $PPP 34,000.

Who are these people, the richest 1 percent of the world (60 million people), who make more than $PPP 34,000 per person annually?[4] Where do they live? Not surprisingly, almost one-half of them are Americans: 29 million to be exact. Next follow about 4 million Germans; about 3 million French, Italians, and Britons each; 2 million Canadians, Koreans, Japanese, and Brazilians each; around 1 million of Swiss, Spaniards, Australians, Dutch, Taiwanese, Chileans, and Singaporeans. There is nobody from Africa, China, India, or from East Europe or Russia (in statistically significant numbers, of course).

At the end, can we estimate the threshold income needed to be part of the one-tenth of 1 percent of the richest people in the world? Now, we move into slippery territory and are very likely to underestimate the amounts needed to qualify for that august position. The reason is that most of the truly rich people simply do not participate in household surveys or intentionally underestimate their incomes. With these caveats in mind, it seems that one needs about $PPP 70,000 annually to be among the 6 million richest people in the world.[5] This is an easy mnemonic: To be among the richest 6 or 7 million people in the world, you need an annual after-tax income of $PPP 70,000 per each member of your household.

For this "top of the world," we may check to see how the Pareto rule that we defined before (see Vignette 1.10) works.

Going from the top 1 percent to the top 0.1 percent means that the number of people is reduced from 60 million to 6 million, while the income threshold goes up by about twice ($PPP 70,000 / $PPP 34,000). The formula gives us the Pareto "guillotine" of about 3.2.[6] This is much more than what Pareto found in the sample of late-nineteenth- and early-twentieth-century European countries (the Pareto "constant" lay between 1.4 and 1.5). We can conclude that the "guillotine of incomes" works much more sharply among the very top of the global income distribution where even a very small increase in "required" income threshold is sufficient to "disqualify" a significant percentage of people. It is slippery at the top . . .

Does the World Have
a Middle Class?

Many people say the world does have a middle class.[1] Impressed
by the high growth rates of China and India, their large populations, and consequently the high number of people with incomes
that made them nationally middle class, they argue that something like a global middle class already exists. But as we shall see,
it is at best only emerging.

If we want to speak of a "global" middle class, we need to define such a class on a global scale following the same rules used
to find out if there is one (and how large it is) nationally. An approach that has become popular recently is to consider as middle class all those with incomes that are within 25 percent of
the national median income.[2] (Median income is the income
that divides a given population into two equal halves: 50 percent
have less than that income and 50 percent have more.) Very unequal countries, with small middle classes, like most countries
in Latin America, have only about 20 percent of their population within these defined limits. In developed countries, the
percentage of the middle class is around 40. Moreover, these
two middle classes are not equally rich (in relation to their
country mean income). In Latin American countries, the middle class has, on average, an income that is about 60 percent of

the national mean. In West Europe, the United States, and Canada, the middle classes' average income is about 85 percent of the national mean.[3] These two numbers (middle-class share and its relative incomes) therefore give us an empirical range between what could be considered a society with a small (and presumably weak) middle class to a fundamentally middle-class society. So how does the world compare with these data?

Not very well. As of 2005 (which is the most recent date for which such global numbers can be produced) the global middle class was composed of 850 million people, which is only slightly less than 15 percent of the world population, and its average income was only 29 percent of the global mean income. However, calling it "middle" in this context is somewhat of a misnomer. The reason lies in the huge inequality that exists in the world that makes the median income in 2005 (as we have seen in the previous vignette) only $PPP 1,225. This is just about $PPP 3.3 per capita per day, one-quarter or less of rich countries' official poverty lines. We shall therefore call this group the global *median* class. It comprises people whose per capita income ranges from $PPP 2.5 to a little more than $PPP 4 per day. In other words, we need to recall that the global median class is indeed a very *poor* class by first world standards. Still, this global median class is much smaller than the middle classes in countries such as Panama and Brazil and also economically much weaker. It receives some 4 percent of the global income versus one-third of the national incomes that middle classes in developed countries receive. To paraphrase Mark Twain, the reports about the rise of the global median, and even more so global *middle*, class have been greatly exaggerated.

But, it could be asked, is this bleak situation perhaps still an improvement over the past? We cannot go far into the past because for this kind of calculation we need to have household-survey data for almost all countries in the world, and they are not available for the period before 1988. Using the same definitions as before, in 1988, the global median class included 13 percent of the world population (its average income being 23 percent of the world mean), in 1993 14 percent of people (average income 26 percent of the global mean), in 1998 17 percent (27 percent of the global mean), and in 2002 15 percent (25 percent of the global mean). Thus, as of 2005, there is no apparent trend in the percentage of people who may be considered the global median class: It oscillates between 13 and 17 percent, and it consistently receives less than 5 percent of the total global income, a far cry indeed from anything we would deem even a modest middle-class society.

As we have seen, in absolute numbers, the global median class can be estimated at 850 million people. This is, of course, a big number, but its global purchasing power is small: It makes (and spends) only 4 to 5 percent of the global income. For comparison, the richest 1 percent of people in the world receive more than 13 percent of the global income. If you are trying to market something, the top group is a much more valuable target since their purchasing power is about three times greater than the purchasing power of the vaunted "global median class."

Most of the global median class is from Asia: a little under 600 million people. Latin America contributes about 90 million and Africa (including North Africa) 100 million. This global median class is predominantly composed of what used to be called the third world. It is revealing that there is an almost total absence of population from developed countries: only some 15 million people. Why? Because none of them is so poor—as obviously implied by the fact that the upper income bound of the global median class is significantly *below* the official poverty threshold used in the rich countries. In effect, people from the rich world who belong to the global median class are all from Turkey—the poorest among the Western nations.[4]

So, if the global median or middle class is so modest in number, why is there so much talk of it? I think there are two reasons for it. First, people are rightly impressed by the economic strides made by China and India. Then, rather unthinkingly, they use these poor countries' standards of what defines a middle class when they speak of a global middle class. They do not sufficiently realize that there is no sense in defining a global middle class by using the yardsticks from the countries that have average incomes that are only one-tenth (China) and one-seventeenth (India) that of the United States. From the popular press, this tendency has then spilled over to scholars. Recently, the global middle class was defined to comprise everybody with incomes between $PPP 2 and $PPP 10 per capita per day.[5] Now, the lower bound of the thus-defined global middle class is less than one-fifth of what is considered to be the poverty level in Western countries, while the upper bound is *lower* than the U.S. poverty line. Does it make sense to proclaim somebody who is almost abjectly poor by Western standards to be a "global middle-class" person?

The second reason is that observers are overly impressed by the greater availability of consumer durables like color televisions and cell phones in poor countries. Due to the technological revolution (there were no cell phones ten years ago) and the decline in relative prices, consumer goods are now available to a lot of people. Far be it from me to deny their value and importance, but a cell phone does not a middle class make. If one lives in a shack, in insalubrious conditions, with a volatile income that is barely above subsistence, and is unable to send his kids to school or offer to his family decent health care, it makes no sense to classify him as part of some imaginary "global middle class" because he can dial a cell phone.[6]

How Different Are the United States and the European Union?

It is an interesting factoid that by 2007, after the latest round of the EU enlargement (as Bulgaria and Romania became members), the overall inequality in the European Union, composed of twenty-seven member countries, and in the United States, composed of fifty states, is about the same. The Gini coefficient in both is just above 40. The United States is, as commonly perceived, more unequal than individual European countries like France, Spain, or Germany, but its inequality is the same as in the EU as a whole.

Yet the underlying structure of these two inequalities is very different. In the European Union 23 points of the total 40 Gini points are due to inequality among the member nations, that is, to the inequality in mean incomes among the countries. But in the United States, fewer than 5 Gini points (out of the same total of 40) are due to the inequalities among average incomes of the states.

Simply put, this means that the main cause of inequality in the EU is that its member countries are different: They are either rich or poor. In the United States, the main cause of inequality is that regardless of state, there are rich and poor people.

They are not, like in Europe, geographically concentrated in some states but dispersed across all fifty of them.

The EU comprises countries that span the spectrum from Luxembourg, the richest country in the world, with a GDP per capita of more than $PPP 70,000, to Romania with a GDP per capita (adjusted for the lower price level in Romania) of only $PPP 10,000. The ratio between the averages is thus 7 to 1. It is not surprising, given that the European within-national income distributions are relatively compressed, that if we divide the populations of Luxembourg and Romania into groups of 5 percent of population each (the "ventiles"), running from the poorest to the richest, the poorest Luxembourgeois ventile would have a much higher income than the richest Romanian ventile. In other words, Luxembourg's and Romania's distributions do not overlap at all: Where Romania's income distribution ends, Luxembourg's income distribution just begins. Practically, this means that *all* Luxembourgeois are richer than *all* Romanians. The situation is not as dramatic but is nevertheless very similar if we compare Denmark or Finland (whose poorest population ventiles are, together with Luxembourg's, the best off in the EU) with countries such as Lithuania and Bulgaria. For example, the poorest people in Denmark are richer than 85 percent of the Bulgarian population.

The picture of inequality in the United States is entirely different. The ratio between the per capita incomes of the richest state (New Hampshire) and the poorest state (Arkansas) is only 1.5 to 1.[1] The average incomes of the states are all very closely bunched together: That can be seen in the almost uniform shade of the United States in the map (page 179) showing relative state GDPs per capita and contrasted with much greater variability of average income exhibited by European Union members. The bunching of mean incomes across the U.S. states, called "convergence," has been going on for the past fifty years.[2] However, each individual state itself is very unequal. The state-level Gini coefficients start at 33 points in South Dakota and Wisconsin (the two most equal states) and end with Texas and Tennessee, whose Gini coefficients are almost at Latin American levels, around 45 Gini points. This is to be contrasted with inequality in European countries that ranges from the most equal, Hungary and Denmark, with Ginis of around 24–25, to the most unequal, Great Britain and Estonia, with Ginis of 37.

In other words, looking at states or countries alone, European high-inequality countries like Great Britain would, in the U.S. context, be considered fairly egalitarian. If it were a U.S. state, Great Britain would rank as the sixteenth most *equal* state. The map on page 180 contrasting inequalities in the two continents shows again an almost uniform dark coloring, indicating high Gini inequality across the United States, and much greater variability as well as generally lower Gini among European Union countries.

In the United States, inequality is a matter of individuals; in the European Union, it is a matter of countries. Consequently, the policies to address inequality and poverty must be different, too. In the United States, social policies must target poor individuals regardless of where they live; in the European Union, social policies (called "cohesion" policies) must target poor countries (or regions like the Mezzogiorno in Italy) because they contain a disproportionate number of poor people.

Which one is better? Is it better to have people with low incomes geographically concentrated or dispersed? Surely, a large discrepancy in mean incomes is hardly a recipe for a successful

INCOME LEVELS
GDP PER CAPITA IN THE UNITED STATES AND EUROPEAN UNION, 2008

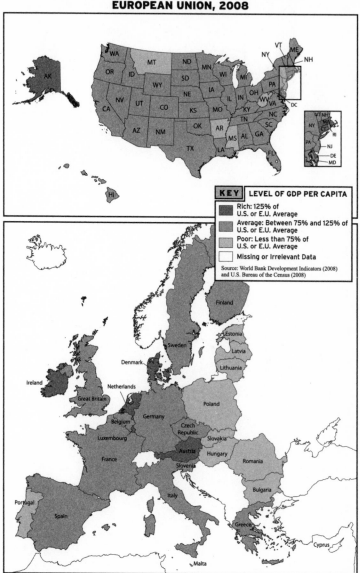

KEY | **LEVEL OF GDP PER CAPITA**

Rich: 125% of U.S. or E.U. Average

Average: Between 75% and 125% of U.S. or E.U. Average

Poor: Less than 75% of U.S. or E.U. Average

Missing or Irrelevant Data

Source: World Bank Development Indicators (2008) and U.S. Bureau of the Census (2008)

INCOME INEQUALITY
IN THE UNITED STATES AND
EUROPEAN UNION, AROUND 2005

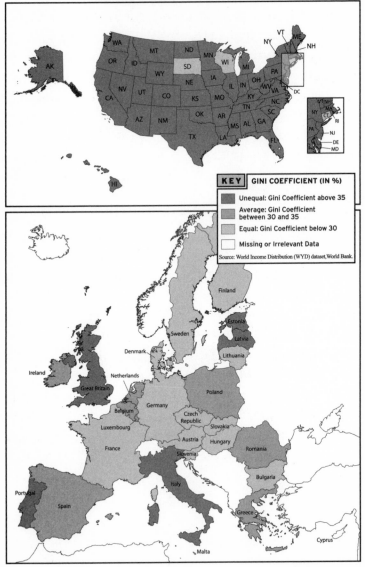

KEY GINI COEFFICIENT (IN %)

Unequal: Gini Coefficient above 35

Average: Gini Coefficient between 30 and 35

Equal: Gini Coefficient below 30

Missing or Irrelevant Data

Source: World Income Distribution (WYD) dataset, World Bank.

union (see Vignette 1.8), especially if it comes atop other characteristics that differentiate people: ethnicity, language, culture, and history. Income cleavage and other cleavages reinforce each other. "Translated" in the U.S. context, it would be as if the income gap that currently reinforces the racial cleavage were to be also geographically concentrated, with populations of poorer states being dominantly African American and that of richer states almost wholly Caucasian.

The European Union framers were aware of the long-run unsustainability of a very economically unequal union, and hence policies have for years been directed toward helping the growth rates of the poorer members. Europe has indeed been successful in raising the incomes of the members that were poorer when they joined. Spain, Portugal, Greece, and Ireland were all, at the time when they joined the Union, poor relative to the Union-wide average. In 1986, when Portugal became a member of the EU, its GDP per capita was 45 percent below the then Union-wide mean. Twenty years later, its GDP per capita is only a third smaller than the Union-wide average (more exactly, the average of the West European members whom Portugal joined in 1986). There is no reason the new eastern members will not catch up within the next generation or two. Free circulation of people, capital, and goods will contribute to this—as much as the free circulation of people, capital, and goods contributed to equalizing the mean incomes of U.S. states between 1950 and now.

Why Are Asia and Latin America Mirror Images of Each Other?

Latin America is a continent composed of internally very unequal countries that, however, do not differ among themselves much in their income levels. Asia is a continent composed of internally relatively equal countries that differ among each other tremendously in terms of their average incomes.[1] This is in a nutshell the contrast between these two continents.

In 2007 GDP per capita in Latin America ranged from the poorest, Nicaragua, at $PPP 2,400, to the richest, Chile, at more than $PPP 13,000. So the range was 5.4 to 1. In Asia the span of incomes went from around $PPP 1,000 in Nepal and Bangladesh to $PPP 47,000 in Singapore and $PPP 40,000 in Hong Kong. Even if we decide to disregard these two city-economies[2] and use the third-richest Asian economy, Japan, with its GDP per capita of $PPP 32,000, the ratio is still 32 to 1. In both cases, these ratios are calculated for incomes expressed in dollars of equal purchasing power ($PPP), which means that they reflect the actual differences in the standard of living of citizens of different countries.

Other more sophisticated measures of inequality tell the same story. In short, of all continents, Asia is the most heterogeneous. It contains very populous countries like Bangladesh (160 million people) and Nepal (almost 30 million), at income levels that are not much beyond the estimated income level of the Roman Empire (see Vignette 1.3). Huge countries like India (1.1 billion people), Pakistan (162 million), Vietnam (85 million), or Burma (48 million) are not much better off, either. Their incomes are just at the level of the poorest Latin American nation, Nicaragua.

But then consider the richest Asian countries: Malaysia is at the same level as the richest Latin American country (Chile), but we still have in Asia five richer countries: the two city-states, Japan (127 million people), South Korea (48 million), and Taiwan (23 million). Thus, the top in Asia extends further than the top in Latin America and the bottom extends much further below and is much "fatter" (in the sense that it contains a large proportion of the Asian population). Even the "miracle" China is at a level of income slightly below El Salvador, and within the Latin American context it would be classified at seventh from the bottom out of twenty-two Latin American countries.

Let us now change the point of view and consider internal inequalities in countries of the two continents. The lowest inequality in Latin America is in Uruguay, with a Gini coefficient of 45; the highest inequality is in Brazil and Bolivia, with Ginis just below 60. Now, in Asia, the least unequal are Japan and Bangladesh, with Ginis slightly below 30, and the most unequal, Hong Kong, with a Gini of 50. The striking fact is that the most equal Latin American country, a rather tiny Uruguay, would be classified as the third most unequal country were it located in Asia! The range of inequality charted by Latin American countries is such that its most equal countries start practically at the point where the most unequal countries in Asia are. The two

Gini spans, Asia (30–50) and Latin America (45–60), hardly overlap at all.

When we put these two things together—(1) huge differences in mean incomes in Asia and small differences in Latin America, as well as (2) huge inequality in incomes within every country in Latin America and relatively equal distributions in Asia—we obtain that inequality across all individuals in Asia and Latin America as a whole is very similar. While (1) helps equality in Latin America, (2) does the opposite. The same mutatis mutandis holds for Asia. The overall Gini for Latin America is 56; the overall Gini for Asia is 60. Notice that the overall Gini for Latin America is very similar to inequality levels in all its countries; in other words, "putting together" Latin America from its component countries is not much different from taking any individual country (at random) and "blowing it up" to the level of the entire Latin America. Either Peru, Argentina, or Bolivia can be about equally representative of Latin America as a whole, whether by its mean income or distribution. But this is not the case for Asia. The Asia-wide inequality is much greater than the inequality in even the most unequal Asian countries. Why? Because when we add together Asian countries with such dissimilar average income levels, the inequality of the whole expands. Taking any country randomly here is likely to lead us very much astray: Bangladesh is not representative of Asia as a whole, nor is South Korea. Since Asian countries are so different in terms of the average income among themselves, there is no country that is "representative" of Asia.

Thus, there is a key difference whence the inequality originates: Most of the Asia-wide inequality is caused by the differences in mean incomes among the nations or, which is the same thing, in their levels of development; in Latin America most of the differences are due to the inequalities within each nation. In the terminology that we have used before (see Vignette 2.1), we can say that the cause of inequality in Latin America is "class," and the cause of inequality in Asia is "location." Latin America gives us a picture of the world as it existed two hundred years ago when top classes' incomes were very similar (and they easily interacted among themselves and acknowledged each other as equals). Asia gives us a picture of today's world with enormous gaps between the countries where citizenship (e.g., of Japan versus Nepal) is a key determinant of one's lifetime income.

Will the distance between these two mirror images of each other be reduced? It is possible, but it will not happen overnight. Poor countries of Asia may begin growing at much higher rates than they have until now, and at higher rates than the rich Asian countries. That would make Asia a more homogenous continent. But this is going to take a very long time. Differently, there could be the emergence of "Latin pumas" that would strongly pull ahead of the rest of Latin America. The continent would thus become more heterogeneous. And at the same time were income inequality within each country to be reduced substantially, Latin America could come to resemble today's Asia (and today's world). But again, such a development seems highly unlikely: Latin American countries have tended to grow at broadly similar rates, no particular "pumas" are in sight, and lowering inequality seems to be a Sisyphean task that many a government in Latin America has tried with very little success. Entrenched interests, large gaps in educational achievement, and racial divides all make such a reduction in inequality difficult to contemplate over the short to medium term.

And let us, at the end, point to one interesting implication of Asian heterogeneity: It probably makes very difficult (or impossible) a continent's closer political union. Even leaving aside the two giants (China and India) that are hard to fit within any specifically Asian political architecture, a closer political union, like the one achieved in Europe, is rendered more difficult by the huge gaps in economic development that exist in Asia. As we have seen before (Vignettes 1.8 and 3.3), for unions to be viable, there should be some broad similarity in living conditions among member states. This cannot be achieved anytime soon in Asia, and any move in that direction would require large aid from the rich countries to the poor. That aid would have to be so large that the cost of closer political union must appear too onerous to the rich countries like Japan, South Korea, and Malaysia even if politically they were to contemplate it. So do not hold your breath to see an Asian Union appear anytime soon!

Do You Want to Know the Winner Before the Game Begins?

Club-level soccer is organized like the purest capitalist enterprise.[1] Unlike U.S. sports where franchises (leagues) impose club rules that are supposed to ensure an overall league competitiveness, in European soccer such rules do not exist. Each club is an independent financial and athletic enterprise. If it is rich, it will be able to buy the best players and will be likely to dominate domestic and European championships. If it is poor, it has no chance whatsoever, its best bet being to identify some young talent that can be sold well to richer clubs.

It has not always been like this. The purely capitalist club rules were tempered by the requirement that only up to two players in a club may be foreigners, that is, nonnationals of the country where the club is located. Thus, AC Milan could play at most two non-Italians, Bayern Munich only two non-Germans, and so forth. This limit came to a crushing end thanks to the so-called *Bosman* court ruling. Jean-Marc Bosman was a Belgian player who in 1995 brought the two-foreigners rule to the attention of the European Court of Justice. The limits on foreign players were in flagrant violation of the EU's commitment to the free circulation of labor among member countries. Why is it that German computer scientists could work in Spain in unlimited numbers but not German soccer players? The ruling thus did away with all limits on the number of foreigners that hailed from other EU member countries. Moreover, it precipitated the relaxation of the rules on soccer players from non-EU countries (mostly from Latin America and Africa), as league after league relaxed or abandoned the limits altogether. Thus, the situation described in the opening paragraph came to be: an unfettered capitalism with full freedom of movement of labor (players and coaches) and capital. The latter is reflected in several famous club acquisitions: Italy's Prime Minister and media tycoon Silvio Berlusconi's ownership of top Italian club AC Milan, Russian oligarch Roman Abramovich's purchase of London Chelsea, former Thai prime minister Thanksin Shriniwatra's investment in Manchester City (subsequently bought out by a conglomerate of rich Arab investors), American billionaires George Gillet and Tom Hicks's acquisition of Liverpool FC, Indian steel magnate Lakshmi Mittel's purchase of the Bulgarian Levski Club—the list could go on and on.

The trend of "globalization" or "delocalization" whereby clubs gradually lose their national and local character but acquire, in terms of players and capital as well as supporters, a global flavor has advanced very far. London's Arsenal or Milan's Inter often do not have a single player on the field, or on the bench, who is respectively English or Italian. Their coaches are foreigners, too.[2] Other clubs are only marginally different: They may have eight or nine foreigners out of eleven players. This has become so common that practically no one notices it anymore (which is in many respects a very good thing).

Soccer clubs have also become global brands. The most well known is Manchester United, which has a huge fan base in Asia (including the Middle East), and a somewhat smaller one in

North America. Every summer Manchester United plays a number of well-paid exhibition matches that from a competitive point of view bring little (if anything) but are supposed to shore up its far-flung fan base. It is a common sight to see Malaysians, Syrians, or Latvians following matches of the top European leagues (English, Italian, Spanish, and German) with a level of interest and attention that is far beyond anything they bestow on domestic clubs and leagues. To keep their foreign fans happy and informed, all major clubs maintain their English-language Web sites as up to date as their Italian and Catalan sites.

The divorce between interest in, and support of, a club and its geographical proximity to the fans is now pervasive. That is, many fans live very, very far from the city where the clubs are located and where they play their home games. It has certain good sides. For example, it diminishes nationalistic, religious, or class passions that in soccer were often linked with particular clubs. But on the negative side is the loss of that intimate connection between fans and players who in the olden days could run into each other in bars or on city streets and feel like they were part of the same community. Today, a Tunisian supporter (if, say, Barcelona rather than the local Esperance has become his favorite team) cannot, short of traveling to Barcelona, ever hope to see Lionel Messi in person, much less run into him in a local bar, but he can follow, in real time, his every dribble and pass.

But here we are concerned with an additional element. Inequality in wealth between the clubs, combined with the removal of the limits on the purchase of foreign players, has led to the concentration of the best players and clubs in the richest countries (adjusted of course for the soccer passion of their populations). Thus, four nations—England, Spain, Italy, and Germany—have come to thoroughly dominate the European club soccer scene, and from each of them it translates into a domination of at most three or four clubs.

The richest clubs, since they are able to buy the best players, are also the "winningest" clubs. One does not need to know much more than the wealths of the two clubs when they play against each other to correctly guess the likely winner. He or she does not need to bother learning which players are playing for the richer and which for the poorer club, how good they are, or in what physical shape. The laws of economics will ensure that the richer club will very likely have better players, or a deeper bench (to be brought in in the case of a top player's injury), or a more astute coach guiding the team.

The top-tier clubs are thus in a category of their own where they collect all, or almost all, championships. The elite European soccer competition is the Champions' League. It has existed (in a somewhat changed format) for more than fifty years, since 1956. It is played annually, and the winner is the European club champion. With the concentration of quality, the number of clubs who have a realistic chance to make it to the quarter finals, the elite eight, is more and more limited and predictable. Some fifteen to twenty of the richest European clubs are the only real candidates; the chances of other clubs are minimal.

And indeed if we look at the five-year averages since the Champions' League began, we see a marked concentration of the elite. Theoretically, if each year there was a different batch of eight clubs in the quarter finals, over each five-year period there would be a maximum of forty different clubs. That would be the case of maximum diffusion of quality, and presumably the highest uncertainty as to the winner. At the other extreme, there could be only eight clubs in the quarter finals, year after year. When we calculate the actual values, we find that between the first five-year period, 1958–1962,[3] and the eighth quinquennium, 1993–1997, that is, forty years, the number of clubs among the elite ranged between twenty-six and thirty. The diffusion of quality was pretty high: almost three-quarters of its maximum value. But after the *Bosman* ruling, in the two most recent five-year periods, that number took a nosedive: It fell to twenty-two in the period 1982–2002 and then further to twenty-one clubs in the most recent period, running from 2003 to 2007.

The same concentration is observed in national competitions. In the past fifteen years, all English soccer championships but one were won by only four clubs, the so-called Big Four: Manchester United, Chelsea, Arsenal, and Liverpool. The concentration is even greater in Italy. Only twice in the last twenty championships has a non-top-four club (that is, different from AC Milan, Juventus, Inter, or Roma) won the prestigious Serie A. It goes almost without saying that the top four Italian clubs, like the top four English clubs, are on the list of the twenty richest European clubs.[4] In Spain, it is Real Madrid and Barcelona that share sixteen out of the last twenty championships. In Germany thirteen out of the last seventeen championships were won by only two clubs: Bayern Munich and Borussia Dortmund. In 2010, more than a year after these lines were written, the national championships were won—yes, you guessed it right—by Chelsea in England, Inter Milan in Italy, Barcelona in Spain, and Bayern Munich in Germany.

Thus, although the quality of soccer is, according to most observers and fans, higher now than ever before—the physical abilities and fitness of today's players being far beyond those of players twenty or thirty years ago, and the tactics and coaching having advanced tremendously—the concentration of wealth and talent, which has probably made this possible, has come at the expense of a loss of excitement. Actually, one of the greatest draws to soccer lay in the unpredictability of its outcomes, its replication of life[5]—namely, the combination of deserved wins of a "better" team with random outcomes where an obviously weaker side would, by a stroke of luck or sudden inspiration, overwhelm a Goliath. Today, as the gap between the Goliaths and Davids is much greater than ever, surprises are much less likely to happen. Goliaths always win; moreover, they often do not deign to play with Davids.

Income Inequality and the Global Financial Crisis

The current financial crisis is generally blamed on feckless bankers, financial deregulation, crony capitalism, and the like.[1] Although all of these elements may have contributed, this purely financial explanation of the crisis overlooks its fundamental reasons. They lie in the real sector, and more exactly in the distribution of income across individuals and social classes. Deregulation, by helping irresponsible behavior, just exacerbated the crisis; it did not create it.

To understand the origins of the crisis, one needs to go to rising income inequality within practically all countries in the world, and the United States in particular, over the past thirty years. In the United States, the top 1 percent of the population doubled its share in national income from around 8 percent in the mid-1970s to almost 16 percent in the early 2000s.[2] That eerily replicated the situation that existed just prior to the crash of 1929, when the top 1 percent share reached its previous high-water mark. American income inequality over the past hundred years thus basically charted a gigantic U, going down from its 1929 peak all the way to the late 1970s, and then rising again for thirty years.

What did the increase mean? Such enormous wealth could not be used for consumption only. There is a limit to the number of Dom Pérignons and Armani suits one can drink or wear. And, of course, it was not reasonable either to "invest" solely in conspicuous consumption when wealth could be further increased by judicious investment. So, a huge pool of available financial capital—the product of increased income inequality—went in search of profitable opportunities in which to invest.

But the richest people and the hundreds of thousands somewhat less rich could not invest the money themselves. They needed intermediaries, the financial sector. Overwhelmed with such an amount of funds, and short of good opportunities to invest the capital as well as enticed by large fees attending each transaction, the financial sector became more and more reckless, basically throwing money at anyone who would take it. Although one cannot prove that investable resources eventually exceeded the number of safe and profitable investment opportunities (since nobody knows a priori how many and where there are good investment opportunities), this is strongly suggested by the increasing riskiness of investments that the financiers had to undertake.

But this is only one part of the equation: how and why large amounts of investable money went in search of a return on that money. The second part of the equation explains who borrowed that money. There again we go back to the rising inequality. The increased wealth at the top was combined with an absence of real economic growth in the middle. The real median wage in the United States has been stagnant for twenty-five years, despite an almost doubling of GDP per capita. About one-half of all real income gains between 1976 and 2006 accrued to the richest 5 percent of households.[3] The new "Gilded Age" was understandably not very popular among the middle class who saw their purchasing power not budge for years. Middle-class income stagnation became a recurrent theme in American political life, and an insoluble political problem for both Democrats and Republicans. Politicians obviously had an interest in making their constituents happy, for otherwise they may not vote for them. Yet they could not just raise their wages. A way to make it seem that the middle class was earning more than it did was to increase its purchasing power through broader and more accessible credit. People began to live by accumulating ever-rising debts on their credit cards, taking on more car debts or higher mortgages. President George W. Bush famously promised that every American family, regardless of its income, would be able to own a home. Thus was born the great American consumption binge that saw the household debt increase from 48 percent of GDP in the early 1980s to 100 percent of GDP before the crisis.

The interests of several large groups of people became closely aligned. High-net-worth individuals and the financial sector were, as we have seen, keen to find new lending opportunities. Politicians were eager to "solve" the irritable problem of middle-class income stagnation. The middle class and those poorer than them were happy to see their tight budget constraints removed as if by a magic wand, consume all the fine things purchased by the rich, and partake in the longest U.S. economic expansion since World War II. Suddenly, the middle class too felt like winners.

This is what more than two centuries ago the great French philosopher Montesquieu mocked when he described the mechanism used by the creators of paper money in France (an experiment that eventually crumbled with a thud): "People of Baetica," wrote Montesquieu, "do you want to be rich? Imagine that I am very much so, and that you are very rich also; every morning tell yourself that your fortune has doubled during the night; and if you have creditors, go pay them with what you have imagined, and tell them to imagine it in their turn."[4]

The credit-fueled system was further helped by the ability of the United States to run large current account deficits, that is, to have several percentage points of its consumption financed by foreigners. The consumption binge also took the edge off class conflict and maintained the American dream of a rising tide that lifts all boats. But it was not sustainable. Once the middle class began defaulting on its debts, the dream collapsed.

We should not focus on the superficial aspects of the crisis, on the arcana of how "derivatives" work. If "derivatives" they were, they were the "derivatives" of the model of growth pursued over the past quarter century. The root cause of the crisis is not to be found in hedge funds and bankers who simply behaved with the greed to which they are accustomed (and for which economists used to praise them). The real cause of the crisis lies in huge inequalities in income distribution that generated much larger investable funds than could be profitably employed. The political problem of insufficient economic growth of the middle class was then "solved" by opening the floodgates of cheap credit. And the opening of the credit floodgates, to placate the middle class, was needed because in a democratic system, an excessively unequal model of development cannot coexist with political stability.

Could it have worked out differently? Yes, without thirty years of rising inequality, and with the same overall national income, the income of the middle class would have been greater. People with middling incomes have many more priority needs to satisfy before they become preoccupied with the best investment opportunities for their excess money. Thus, the structure of consumption would have been different: Probably more money would have been spent on home-cooked meals than on restaurants, on near-home vacations than on exotic destinations, on kids' clothes than on designer apparel. More equitable development would have removed the need for the politicians to look around in order to find palliatives with which to assuage the anger of their middle-class constituents. In other words, there would have been more equitable and stable development that would have spared the United States and the world an unnecessary crisis.

Did Colonizers Exploit as Much as They Could?

The main measure of inequality, as we have seen before, is the Gini coefficient.[1] Its value runs from a theoretical value of 0, when the entire income (of a country, community, continent, world—whatever our unit of observation is) is divided among people exactly equally, to a theoretical maximum value of 100, when the entire income is appropriated by one person and all others have zero incomes. But obviously people cannot live at a zero income (or consumption) for any period of time, much less for a year, which is the conventional unit of time over which inequality (and the Gini coefficient) are measured. Let us thus introduce the constraint that all members of a society have at least the physiological subsistence minimum, for otherwise people would die and society would shrink and disappear. We can then calculate the maximum inequality (Gini) a society can attain under that constraint. The derivation of the maximum Gini assumes that all members of society but a tiny elite live at the subsistence income and that the tiny elite (whose number at the extreme may consist of only one person) appropriates the entire difference between the total income and what is needed for everybody else to live merely at the subsistence level.

A moment of reflection should make it clear that if a society has a very low average income, regardless of how tiny the ruling elite is, measured inequality cannot be very high. To see this, assume that a society's average income is just a fraction above subsistence. The income that remains for the elite will also be extremely low, and inequality measures, which in principle take into account the incomes differences between all individuals (see Essay I), cannot be very high simply because in 99.99 percent of cases (for all these people living at the subsistence level), the pairwise income comparisons between these individuals will be zero. As the average income increases, this binding constraint on inequality is relaxed, and the maximum Gini can be greater. When we chart a curve (see the full line in Figure 7 below) that links the maximum feasible Ginis to alternative average incomes, we get an upward sloping curve, concave from below, that approaches the maximum Gini value of 100 as the average income becomes many times greater than subsistence. That curve is called the Inequality Possibility Frontier (IPF).[2] To give concrete numbers, if the average income of a society is twice the subsistence, then the maximum Gini (the "frontier") will be 50. If the average income is three times the subsistence, the "frontier" Gini will be 66. And so forth: If the average income is 100 times greater than the physiological subsistence, which is the case in today's rich countries, then the maximum feasible Gini is 99.

This concept is important because it shows that in order to sustain high inequality, societies must be relatively rich. We can use the IPF to contrast actual inequality in different preindustrial (as well as modern) societies with their "frontier inequality." If a society is close to its maximum feasible inequality, then the conclusion will be that the elite is very rapacious and exploitative, able,

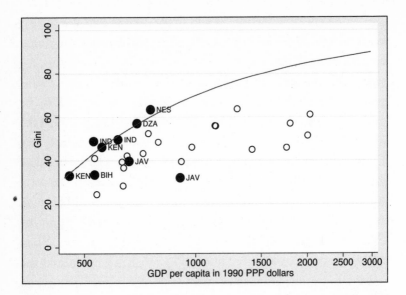

FIGURE 7 Actual and "frontier" Gini for colonies and other preindustrial societies

Notes: The Inequality Possibility Frontier shows the maximum inequality (Gini) on the vertical axis that is theoretically achievable at a given average income (shown on the horizontal axis) under the constraint that income of no member of society may be below the subsistence minimum. Colonies are indicated by full dots, other preindustrial societies by hollow dots. KEN = Kenya, BIH = Bihar, IND = India, JAV = Java, DZA = Maghreb, NES = Nueva España (Mexico and the Southwest of the United States).
Source: Milanovic, Lindert, and Williamson, *Measuring Ancient Inequality*.

by force or guile, to appropriate for itself the entire surplus over the physiological minimum. If the actual inequality is far from the frontier, the elite is moderate, or is prevented from extracting more surplus. Obviously, this approach will be particularly fruitful when we study preindustrial societies, not only because their elites are thought to have been more predatory but also because at their (low) income levels the inequality frontier was much more binding. The ratio between the actual and "frontier" inequality is called the "inequality extraction ratio." The closer its value to 100, the more "efficient" the elite is in extracting all the surplus.

In a study of thirty preindustrial economies (covering the period from the early Roman Empire in the year 14 to India in 1947, and including, for example, England in 1209, 1688, 1759, and 1801–1803), Milanovic, Lindert, and Williamson find the average extraction ratio to have been around 75 percent. This is about twice as high as in today's United States, where the Gini coefficient is 40 and the frontier Gini is almost 100. But what is interesting is that, in this sample of thirty societies, there are six where the extraction ratio is around 100 percent. These six societies are Moghul India in 1750, Nueva España (Mexico) in 1790, Maghreb in 1880, Kenya in 1914 and 1927, and India in 1947. Now, what these six cases share in common is that they were all colonies. There are nine colonies in the sample, and the three others (Bihar in 1807 and Java in 1880 and 1924) have extraction ratios that are around 70 percent (see Figure 7).[3] We can conclude that six out of nine colonies appear to have pushed "the art of exploitation" to its extreme, and that all societies where we observe such high exploitation ratios were colonies. The nationality of the colonial master does not seem to matter much because among the six most exploitative societies we find colonies that belonged to the British, French, Moghuls, and Spaniards.

It does not come as a surprise that colonizers were keen and obviously able (for a while at least) to extract maximum surplus from the native populations. What is more shocking is to observe how high were, even in today's terms, the estimated incomes of the colonizer elites. In Java in 1880 the richest Europeans (mostly the Dutch) enjoyed a per capita income in excess of $PPP 200,000 per year.[4] That would easily place them in the top one-tenth of 1 percent of world income distribution *today* (see Vignette 3.1). Similarly, in Kenya in 1914, the top British who accounted for 0.04 percent of the population received 1.4 percent of the total national income, each "rewarded" to the tune of around $PPP 100,000 annually. They too would be part of the top one-tenth of 1 percent of global income distribution today. Moreover, they would also be in the top 1 percent of the British income distribution today.[5] Only slightly less rich were the top British living in Kenya in 1927: about $PPP 74,000 per capita per year (see also Vignette 2.6). They too would find their place in the top UK income percentile today.

So the colonizers were exceedingly rich, not solely in terms of their own time and place but even in terms of their own countries' income distributions today. They extracted as much inequality and surplus as they could, but their "pleasure" could not go on forever. Their rule eventually came to an end. However, in a less sanguine vein, we have to note that the native elites that succeeded them often continued with the same or similar policies of maximum exploitation. Thus, in a number of African countries today, we find Ginis that are approaching the Inequality Possibility Frontier. Examples include Niger, Mozambique, and Guinea-Bissau. In some places the extent of exploitation did not change even if the nationality of the rulers did.

Why Was Rawls Indifferent to Global Inequality?

To those who know John Rawls through his *A Theory of Justice*, the question in this vignette's title may come as a surprise. After all, Rawls is rightly associated with what may be considered a strongly egalitarian position. That position, formulated in his celebrated "difference principle"—which says that the justification for any departure from equality can be found only if such inequality is needed to raise the absolute position (income) of the poorest—holds, however, only at the level of a single nation. How to achieve fairness within a nation was the topic of Rawls's *Theory of Justice*. But in a much later work, *The Law of Peoples*, published in 1999, Rawls went further and addressed the issues of global governance and global justice. There Rawls, at times explicitly and at times implicitly, discussed global income inequality and global income redistribution and rejected the application of the "difference principle" globally. Globally, the difference principle would have implied that any increase in global inequality would have to be justified by arguing that it made the world's poorest better off.

Before we move to the question of global income distribution proper, it is worth looking at Rawls's attitude toward migration. This is important because we have argued earlier that migration stems from great differences in average income levels between countries as well as from better knowledge of these differences and lower transportation costs, both brought about by the process of globalization (see Vignettes 2.3–2.5). Rawls, however, reduces migration to the right of hospitality and asylum given to people who are fleeing political or religious persecution. The most common causes of migration, economic causes—after all, so characteristic for many citizens of the United States (and, one would venture, perhaps even Rawls's own ancestors)—are explicitly rejected:

> The asset is people's territory and its capacity to support them in perpetuity and the agent is the people themselves as politically organized. . . . [T]hey [the people who are poor] are to recognize that they cannot make up for their irresponsibility in caring for their land and its natural resources by conquest in war or by migrating into other people's territory without their consent.[1]

Increasing obstacles to migration raised by rich countries would be, one is led to believe, viewed as fully justified by Rawls. As the passage shows, each people is regarded as a custodian of its own culture, traditions, and piece of land it occupies. As such, each people has the right to accept or exclude members of other peoples from moving in. Thus, one of the potentially key levers for equalization in worldwide living conditions—migration— would be permanently shut off by Rawls.

But Rawls's lack of concern with global inequality goes further. International aid is approved and advocated only if it is needed to help "burdened societies" reach the level of "well-ordered peoples." Let us explain the two terms. "Burdened societies" are those that, for historical reasons, have a low level of income that prevents them from establishing legitimate rules of political conduct and respect for essential human rights. The last two elements plus peaceful behavior toward other peoples define a "well-ordered" people. In such cases, and only in such cases, when becoming "well-ordered" is made impossible by generalized poverty, it is a duty of liberal peoples to help "burdened societies." The help continues only up to a point when "burdened societies" are no longer constrained by material poverty to provide legitimate governance and essential human rights.[2] After that point the duty of assistance ceases.

Once "burdened" societies are transformed into "well-ordered societies," differences in income levels between the nations are no longer of any relevance. This is stated clearly: "Once . . . all peoples have a working liberal or decent government, there is . . . no reason to narrow the gap between average wealth of different peoples."[3] In effect, Rawls believes that such differences in income are the outcome of differences in collective preferences: Some "well-ordered" societies may prefer to save more rather than spend; others may also prefer to work harder rather than enjoy more leisure. Consequently, the outcomes may differ: Some societies will be richer than others. Fundamentally, these differences are immaterial, since the level of wealth a society reaches is reflective of its social choices.[4]

Rising inequality of mean incomes among countries (income divergence), which we have noted (see Vignettes 2.1 and 2.2), would therefore be quite acceptable—so long as we agree that all countries are "well-ordered." Perhaps Rawls would have agreed that many of the very poorest countries in the world are indeed "burdened" and should be helped financially by the rich world (and to that extent would have been concerned by income divergence), but he certainly would not have regarded income divergence among "well-ordered" countries as a problem. Both India and the United States are "well-ordered" societies. Thus, any assistance to India is redundant, since its material poverty simply reflects Indians' social choices. This is stated explicitly by Joshua Cohen, one of the most influential Rawlsian scholars: "Once we accept the value of collective self-government, there is no reason to hope for convergence in living standards—the absence of convergence is not a defect awaiting correction."[5]

Rawls's position is rooted in two interlinked assumptions: (1) Political institutions ("working liberal government," that is, political institutions that will take the interests of all into account) and the observance of basic human rights are really what matter, and (2) acquisition of wealth, as an individual or societal objective, is rejected. In (2), he obviously departs from most economists and the prevalent common wisdom.

It is clear that if migration is not to take place in any massive way, and mean incomes among countries are "allowed" to diverge, global inequality—even if the world fully adhered to the Rawlsian rules enunciated in *The Law of Peoples*—would not look much different from what it is now. The only difference may concern within-national income inequalities. For these, the rules from *Theory of Justice* apply. These rules say, as we saw above, that justification for inequality may be found only if it is necessary to raise the absolute income of the poorest members. We could, for example, argue that the currently existing inequalities in (say) the United States, France, China, or Russia have gone beyond that point and that in a Rawlsian world, they would have to be reduced. So let within-national inequalities everywhere become less. But from our earlier discussion of global in-equality we know that within-national inequalities explain only a small fraction of global interpersonal inequality (10 to 20 per-cent at most, depending on the inequality measure we use). Thus, even if inequalities in all countries of the world (individu-ally) were reduced to some of the lowest levels ever recorded, global inequality would be cut by only a few percentage points. To push this example even further, to somewhat absurd lengths, assume that all within-national inequalities are zero. Every per-son in the world has the mean income of his or her country. We know exactly what would then be a global "Rawlsian" inequality (remember that it would leave intact differences in mean country incomes): Global inequality would amount to 63 rather than 70 Gini points. Thus, even under this utterly implausible scenario, global inequality would be reduced by only 10 percent. The rea-son, of course, is that the main drivers of global inequality today are differences in between-country incomes, and no limit on these is set by Rawls.

This is why neither income divergence nor very high global inequality as such would be frowned upon by Rawls. It could be that our interpretation is too harsh, or that Rawls, faced with the facts of global inequality that were not widely known or ap-preciated when he wrote *The Law of Peoples*, might have recon-sidered his position. But his writings do not allow us to make this conclusion.

Vignette 3.9

Geopolitics in Light of
(or Enlightened by) Economics

Between the end of the Second World War and the fall of the
Berlin Wall, a rather comfortable intellectual division of the
world held sway. There were, as we all knew, three worlds on this
planet. There was the first world of rich capitalist economies.
Not all of them were at the time democracies, but gradually became so (e.g., with political liberalizations in Greece, Spain, Portugal); not all of them were Western: Japan seemed a permanent
big exception.

There was a second world, although, strangely enough, the
term was not frequently used. It existed rather implicitly: Since
there were the first and the third worlds, there must have been
a second, too. The second world was the world of socialist
economies with single-party regimes. They, of course, never re-
ferred to themselves as such (the second world) since they believed themselves to be rather at the vanguard of social change
in the world, and thus in some sense ahead of everybody else
even if they could not claim to be richer than the Western capitalist countries.

Then there was the third world. Unlike the first two, it was a
much more heterogeneous world. It included giants such as India
and tiny countries like Chad. It included rather well-developed

Brazil and poor Nepal. It included ancient civilizations like Egypt and new lands like Papua New Guinea. It covered in principle the three "southern" continents: Latin America, Asia, and Africa. It was to a large extent negatively defined, that is, by what it was not—it was not Europe, and it was not the United States, and it was not the Soviet Union—rather than by what it was. Perhaps the third world countries shared the fact that many were ruled for a century or more by the Europeans and acquired their independence after World War II, although again there were big exceptions: Latin American independence is almost 150 years "older," and some third world countries, like Thailand, were never colonized.

The position of China was then, as now, special and . . . apart. Although during the Maoist times, it supported, sometimes strongly, at least verbally, third world countries, China officially never joined any of the specifically third world organizations like the Non-Aligned Movement or the Group of 77. Perhaps it was distracted by its competition with the Soviet Union on who was "the most socialist" (*¿qui es mas socialista?*); perhaps it was because of its size, which paradoxically discouraged China from being too active lest it provoke suspicions of attempts to dominate the third world movement. Or, perhaps, as we can now speculate, based on more recent experience, China just elected not to play a global role commensurate with its objective importance due to some deeper historical inhibitions.

This "tripartite" view of the world—however inadequate in some particular cases[1]—was by and large not unreasonable and allowed us to organize, at least mentally, the world in a rather tidy fashion. It also corresponded broadly to a division in economic policies followed by the countries. The first world was capitalist but not monolithic. There were welfare-oriented central and North European countries and the more private-sector-dominated United States. The second world's distinguishing characteristic was state ownership of the means of production, but heterogeneity existed there, too, between the centrally planned Soviet Union, on the one hand, and market-oriented Yugoslavia, on the other. The third world, it could be easily averred, was dominated by "developmentalist" policies, where the state played an active role, not only in taxation and spending (as in many Western economies) but also in production. State-led development and import substitution were guiding principles in countries as diverse as Brazil, Turkey, India, Tanzania, and Ghana.

The tripartite classification finally, and perhaps most importantly, correlated also with income levels of the "member countries." In 1975, which may be seen as the high-water mark of this tripartite division of the world (just before the second oil crisis, the debt crisis of the 1980s, and China's takeoff), the first world was composed of countries whose GDP per capita ranged from less than $PPP 10,000 (Portugal) to $PPP 27,000 (Switzerland).[2] The second world was notably poorer, its upper income range hardly outstripping the bottom range of the first world. The income span in the second world went from less than $PPP 2,000 in the central Asian republics of the Soviet Union to $PPP 14,000 in Slovenia and the Czech Republic. The third world consisted of a number of countries whose incomes were close to the subsistence level, that is, below $PPP 500 (including China and many sub-Saharan countries), while at its upper bound—abstracting from small oil-producing countries—were Algeria and South Korea at $PPP 4,000 per capita or somewhat richer Mexico and Brazil at around $PPP 7,000.[3] So, in summary, we had the following distribution of GDPs per capita: the first world (10,000–27,000), the second (2,000–14,000), and the third (400–7,000). Despite some obvious overlap, it was again a rather neat partition, much more neat than anything that we can, with such parsimony, devise today.

This classification exploded in the 1990s. Not only did the second world cease to exist as many of its members joined the first world—most obviously when ten former communist countries became members of the European Union and others joined NATO, a par excellence first world institution—but the third world also largely ceased to exist. The economic rise of Pacific Asia, spreading from Japan to Singapore to South Korea to Taiwan, then to Malaysia, increased wealth in these regions to the level of advanced Western countries. These countries became practically a part of the first (rich) world. They also developed institutions (democracy) similar to those existing in the first world. In addition, China's economic rise combined with the ascendance of Deng Xiaoping and his conservative successors who showed a marked lack of interest in "typical" third world issues further undermined the cohesiveness of the third world. India, too, became much more economically than ideologically minded. It did not seem clear any longer what the third world countries may have in common, and the Non-Aligned Movement, so active in the past, became moribund. Issues of economic growth (or lack of it), religious cleavages, and regional tensions now visibly replaced the erstwhile, always more proclaimed than real, third world solidarity.

So, in what rough categories can we divide the world in the first decade of the twenty-first century? There is still, of course, the first world. It has now became much wider, as it has co-opted some former members from the second and third worlds. The second world is no more, but there is Russia, whose objective is to play in the Eurasian space, among the countries that have not been integrated in the first world, a role analogous to that of France in its former African colonies. Then there are Arab countries that, divided among themselves into the haves and the have-nots (the division being entirely based on the accidental factor of possession of oil), can hardly be seen as a bloc.

Perhaps it is only Latin America that remains in some ways the exemplar of the third world of the past. It is, like the third world of the 1960s and 1970s, the only region that attempts to apply economic policies that are a bit different from the mainstream Western ways. There is a certain coherence to the almost simultaneous emergence of politicians like Nestor Kirchner, Lula de Silva, Evo Morales, and Hugo Chávez. This Latin America, which reaped so few benefits from Globalization 2.0, is thus not surprisingly the only part of the world that is trying to experiment with alternative policies. By the standards of the past, these alternatives are rather meek, since the differences are not in the substance but in the details. But as the world has, in terms of economic policies followed by different countries, become much more homogeneous, even these small departures from the Washington consensus orthodoxy attract attention.

Africa, of course, has remained the third world. But on account of its almost unrelieved misery and relative and often absolute decline during the last quarter of the twentieth century, we may be justified in giving it the unenviable title of the fourth world.

China remains a world apart, with obviously a much higher income today than before but with equally opaque ambitions or rather the same inner ambivalence not only about the role it wants to play internationally but whether it wants a role at all. One of the striking features is that the incredible economic rise of China that was achieved by using a mixture of recipes never seen before, and indeed very different from the recipes (economic policies) advocated by the Washington consensus, has not produced any "codified" rules of economic conduct. There is no attempt to "package" these policies, explain how they might work elsewhere, in other words "sell" a specifically Chinese model of development or economic ideology. Contrast this with the fact that, already by 1776 when the Industrial Revolution was as old as the Chinese "takeoff" is today, the world had in Adam Smith's *Wealth of Nations* well-codified rules for economic success. In Smith's immortal words, "Little else is requisite to carry a state to the highest degree of affluence . . . but peace, easy taxes, and a tolerable administration of justice."[4] We have nothing similar— more exactly almost *nothing*—coming out of China or from the non-Chinese scholars who work in China or believe they understand China's economic miracle. It would all seem to have been a product of a series of serendipitous, unique, and unrepeatable circumstances or accidents not linked by any grand idea. Just a *tâtonnement*, experimentation, and a few lucky strikes. Perhaps it was so. But if a country pretends (or wants) to have a worldwide influence, it must not only sell toys and video recorders but also offer the world an ideology, a way of doing things. China has so far proved incapable or unwilling to do so. Unless it is able to present a compact set of lessons to be taken away from its success, its ideological influence will remain limited.

Attempting any classification today is difficult primarily because of the heterogeneity of Asia (a topic that was addressed in Vignette 3.4). Asia is composed of first world countries like Japan, South Korea, Taiwan, and Singapore; two still very poor giants that defy easy classification (India and China); and a lot of extremely poor countries, some of which are trying to replicate the successes of Japan and South Korea (Thailand, Indonesia), and others that seem to belong, by their income and economic lethargy, to the fourth world (Burma, Cambodia, Laos). If we were to attempt an economic classification, we would have to "let" some parts of Asia go with the rich world, and others, no less important, with the fourth world. Yet there is obviously very little in common between the poor Asian and African countries: Unlike the third world of yore, they have never tried to establish common interests or policies, much less create a bloc of poor nations.

Other continents are (as we saw already) easier to classify. All of Europe (with the exception of Russia) will, it seems, eventually become part of the European Union, and thus be "reattached" to the first world. The most important challenge in this century will be to have economic progress in Africa, for otherwise the continent will increasingly fall in almost all respects behind the rest of the world and look "unabsorbable." Europe should, in principle, play a key role in Africa's development, because of its geographical proximity, historical links, and the successful experience of the European Union's own absorption of poorer members. To be sure, the differences between African countries and those European nations that were successfully integrated into the Union are huge. Yet some form of advanced political and economic partnership between the EU and sub-Saharan Africa could be envisaged, were it not for the so obvious "enlargement fatigue" evinced by the European Union, lack of vision among its leaders, and fundamental doubts among Europeans about their own ability to face and prosper in a globalized world that would embrace free movement of not only capital and goods but people as well (see Vignettes 2.4 and 2.5).

Thus, Africa will have to prosper or fail by its own devices—which, were the former to happen, would be a good thing, since one's own generated success is probably more difficult to overturn. However, proponents of the view that Africa is set back by aid and too much ostensible concern of outsiders, and would be better off if left alone, must acknowledge the fact that the successes of West Europe, East Asia, and South Europe were grounded in the political willingness of other countries to help them develop.[5] In the former two cases, it was U.S. encouragement of open trade and the emphasis on economic recovery that was to serve as a bulwark against communism that helped countries like Japan and South Korea, as well as West Europe, to become rich.[6] In the latter case (South Europe, and very likely East Europe, too) it was the integration into the rich club of the EU. Reasoning by analogy, Africa too would have to be, at first, pulled along. And, except for Europe, it is difficult to see who else could do that, for the Chinese role—despite the recent attention that its investments in Africa have attracted—is likely to remain limited for all the ideological reasons mentioned above and China's still comparative economic poverty.

The key challenges of the twenty-first century may be summarized as follows: how to bring Africa up, how to peacefully bring China in, and how to wean Latin America off of its self-obsession and bring it into the real world. And doing all of this while maintaining peace and avoiding ideological crusades.

But a century ago, Constantine Cavafy wrote:[7]

Men have knowledge of the present.
As for the future, the gods know it,
alone and fully enlightened.

Notes

Preface

1. This statement needs to be qualified though: it applies to *recorded* human history, that is since the introduction of sedentary agriculture. It is thought that during most of pre-recorded history (which accounts for more than 90 percent of total human history), people lived in groups in which equality was quasi absolute (see Ken Binmore, "The Origins of Fair Play," Keynes Lecture 2006, *The Papers on Economics and Evolution*, No. 0614, (Jena: Max Planck Institute, 2006).

Essay 1

1. I am grateful to Francisco Ferreira for very helpful comments on this essay.

2. All landlords with land of better quality than the marginal land would then receive higher rents.

3. See "Response by Thomas Piketty and Emmanuel Saez to: 'The Top 1% . . . of What' by Alan Reynolds," available at http://www.econ.berkeley.edu/~saez/answer-WSJreynolds.pdf.

4. This analogy was first made by Francisco Ferreira, "Inequality as Cholesterol," in *Poverty in Focus* (Brasilia: International Poverty Center, June 2007).

5. Max Weber, *The Protestant Ethic and the Spirit of Capitalism* (reprint, London: Routledge, 1992), 53.

6. J. M. Keynes, *The Economic Consequences of the Peace* (1920; reprint, New York: Penguin, 1971), chap. 2, pt. 3 (emphasis in the original).

7. Stefan Zweig, *The World of Yesterday* (Lincoln: University of Nebraska Press, 1964), 7–8.

8. This is the so-called median-voter hypothesis developed by Kevin Roberts, "Voting over Income Tax Schedules," *Journal of Public Economics* 8 (1977): 329–340, and Allan Meltzer and Scott Richard, "A Rational Theory of the Size of Government," *Journal of Political Economy* 89 (1981): 914–927.

9. It could even happen that there is no real redistribution but that the effects on growth still remain negative. For example, in order to prevent the political

takeover by the poor, the rich can combine and through lobbying buy votes and legislation, thus preventing the redistribution. But this effort at lobbying, a non-productive activity par excellence (because it is a zero-sum game, concerned only with redistribution and not creation of new wealth), will be a sheer waste from the point of view of economic growth, and a slower growth will ensue again.

10. See Oded Galor, "Income Distribution and the Process of Development," *European Economic Review* 44 (2002): 706–712; and Oded Galor and Omer Moav, "From Physical to Human Capital Accumulation: Inequality and the Process of Development," *Review of Economic Studies* 71 (2004): 1001–1026.

11. "He" in this dialogue is Adeimanus, Socrates' older brother.

12. Plato, *The Republic*, translated by Desmond Lee (New York: Penguin, 1973), pt. IV, sec. 3, p. 189.

13. "On the Measurement of Inequality," *Journal of Economic Theory* 2 (1970).

14. Amartya Sen, "Equality of What?" Tanner Lecture on Human Values, delivered at Stanford University, May 22, 1979, available at http://www.tanner lectures.utah.edu/lectures/sen80.pdf. See also Amartya Sen, "Social Justice and the Distribution of Income," in vol. 1 of *Handbook of Income Distribution*, edited by A. B. Atkinson and F. Bourguignon (Amsterdam: Elvesier, 2000).

15. Sen's approach is precisely such: The requirement of equality for all is defined in the space of capabilities, not any longer in the space of utilities.

16. Some economists believe that we can make interpersonal utility comparisons by assuming that people also have, in addition to their own utility scales, empathic utility scales such that they can "measure" the utility enjoyed by others. Empathic and individual utility scales may differ in the precise values that they assign, but they would be "transitive" (if one knows the one, he also knows the other), much like, for instance, Celsius and Fahrenheit scales. The idea goes back to John Harsanyi, "Cardinal Welfare, Individualistic Ethics, and the Inter-personal Comparisons of Utility," *Journal of Political Economy* 63 (1955): 309–321.

17. John Rawls, *A Theory of Justice*, rev. ed. (Cambridge: Harvard University Press, 1999), 13.

18. Ibid., 54.

19. Rawls indirectly excluded the situation where the absolute improvements are realized by both the rich and the poor (thus satisfying his difference principle) while those in the middle of income distribution lose. He thought that income distribution would move like a single interconnected chain (see the definition of "close knittedness" in chap. 2, sec. 13).

20. "And nothing changes" includes the fact that the richer person still remains richer, for otherwise the two could just trade places, and if so, it would be unfair to argue that inequality went down.

Notes

21. The last axiom, though, is not so obvious or innocuous. Note that it implies that the measure does not change even if absolute differences in income between people increase. Measures of inequality that obey this axiom are called "relative," and most measurement uses only such measures. Yet absolute measures (which would increase as the absolute differences in income go up) cannot be totally discounted.

22. Corrado Gini, "Measurement of Inequality of Incomes," *Economic Journal* (March 1921): 124.

23. Latin America and East Europe are in a better position. Reliable surveys in both started in the 1960s. Unfortunately, many of them have been lost, and only a few overall statistical measures remain. The old, and lost, Latin American surveys remind us of Márquez's Macondo, where the past slowly recedes behind the veil of mist and fog until it becomes a myth. Just a few artifacts (one or two aggregate statistics) remain.

24. The same thing can be done with household consumption instead of income. We then say that we are interested in household "welfare"—how much they have really consumed—rather than in household income, that is, how much they could have potentially consumed.

25. The two sums are equal.

26. According to Michele Zenga ("Il contributo degli italiani allo studio della concentrazione: Prima parte: Dal 1895 al 1915," in *La distribuzione personale del reddito: Problemi di formazione, di ripartizione e di misurazione*, edited by M. Zenga [Milan: Vita e Pensiero, 1987], 307–328), the concentration ratio, later dubbed the Gini coefficient, was first introduced in Gini's article "Sulla misura della concentrazione e della variabilità dei caratteri," published in 1914 in *Atti del Reale Istituto Veneto di Scienze, Lettere ed Arti* (Venice: Premiate Officine Grafiche Carlo Ferrari, 1914), vol. 73, pt. 2a, pp. 1203–1248. I am thankful to Andrea Brandolini for this information.

27. Based on Bureau of the Census data for total disposable income from Andrea Brandolini and Tim M. Smeeding, "Inequality Patterns in Western Democracies: Cross-Country Differences and Changes over Time," in *Democracy, Inequality, and Representation: A Comparative Perspective*, edited by Pablo Beramendi and Christopher J. Anderson (New York: Russell Sage Foundation, 2008), fig. 2.5. See also a detailed study by Richard V. Burkhauser et al., *Estimating Trends in U.S. Income Inequality Using the Current Population Survey: The Importance of Controlling for Censoring*, Working Paper 14247 (Cambridge, MA: National Bureau of Economic Research, August 2008).

Vignette 1.1

1. I am grateful to Michele de Nevers, Carol Leonard, and Blanca Sanchez Alonso for comments.

2. A modern commentator thus defines the implications of an income of two thousand pounds in Jane Austen's books: "At two thousand pounds a year (the landed-gentry income of Mr. Bennet in *Pride and Prejudice* and of Colonel Brandon in *Sense and Sensibility*), domestic economy must still hold a tight rein, especially in *Pride and Prejudice* where there are five daughters in need of dowry. . . . Mrs. Jennings in *Sense and Sensibility* emphasizes the quiet, at-home pleasures of £2000 a year when she describes Colonel Brandon's Delaford as 'without debt or drawback: every thing, in short, that one could wish for . . . Oh, 'tis a nice place'" (Edward Copeland, "Money," in *The Cambridge Companion to Jane Austen*, edited by Edward Copeland and Juliet McMaster [Cambridge: Cambridge University Press, 1997], 156).

3. His wealth is £200,000, a conventional rate of return being 4–5 percent per annum.

4. Based on Robert Colquhoun's social tables.

Vignette 1.2

1. I have greatly benefited from the extensive comments of Natalia Drozdova Petrova.

2. *Anna Karenina* (New York: The Modern Library, 2000. Constance Garnett translation revised by Leonard Kent and Nina Berberova), 813.

3. Ibid., 745.

4. Ibid., 347.

5. This is based on the interpretation of Vronsky's conversation with his brother (pt. 5, chap. 13) and his subsequent increase in spending.

6. This assumes that Anna's son (that she has with Mr. Karenin) stays with the father, while the daughter (that she has with Count Vronsky) lives with them.

7. We learn this indirectly: first, because she lives with her rich aunt (presumably, much richer than her parents) and, second, because her marriage to Karenin is a big step forward socially.

8. We do not learn much about the incomes of the middle classes from Tolstoy. The only "professional" income mentioned in the book is that of a German bookkeeper who earns five hundred rubles annually. He must have been paid more than an equivalent Russian bookkeeper (hence the emphasis on "German"), and assuming that he had a family of four people to maintain, the per capita income of such a "middle-class" family may be put at slightly more than one hundred rubles.

Notes

Vignette 1.3

1. Adam Smith, *Wealth of Nations* (New York: Pelican Books, 1970), 133.

2. Aldo Schiavone, *The End of the Past: Ancient Rome and the Modern West* (Cambridge: Harvard University Press, 2000), 71. *Sestercius* means "semithird," indicating its value of two-and-a-half asses (another Roman coin unit).

3. Raymond Goldsmith, in "An Estimate of the Size and Structure of the National Product of the Early Roman Empire," *Review of Income and Wealth* 30 (September 1984), estimates Augustus's annual income at 15 million HS, which, using the conventional interest rate of 6 percent per year, translates into a fortune of 250 million sesterces.

4. Tacitus, *Annals* (New York: Penguin, 1996), bk. 12, chap. 53. Pallas helped Nero in many of his misdeeds until he too was, Tacitus writes, poisoned on Nero's orders (bk. 14, chap. 65).

5. Goldsmith, "Estimate of the Size and Structure." This was estimated by Branko Milanovic, Peter Lindert, and Jeffrey Williamson in "Preindustrial Inequality" (*Economic Journal*, forthcoming; previous version published as *Measuring Ancient Inequality*, National Bureau of Economic Research Working Paper 13550 [National Bureau of Economic Research, October 2007]) to have amounted to a GDP per capita in 1990 international prices of $PPP 633 (PPP stands for "purchasing power parity"; see Essay II). Angus Maddison's estimate is somewhat lower, $PPP 570 (*Contours of the World Economy, 1–2003 AD* [Oxford: Oxford University Press, 2007], chap. 1).

6. This is simply given as an example. The Colosseum was built under Titus, more than one hundred years after Crassus died.

7. According to the *New York Times* obituary from 1937 and Wikipedia. Alan Nevins says the amount did not exceed $900 million (*Study in Power: John D. Rockefeller, Industrialist and Philanthropist*, 2 vols. [New York: Charles Scribner's Sons, 1953], 404–405).

8. *Fortune*'s 2004 list of billionaires.

Vignette 1.4

1. Goldsmith, "An Estimate of the Size and Structure" (see Vignette 1.3, note 3).

2. Ibid., based on Colquhoun's social tables and Lee Soltow's calculations, "Long-run changes in British income inequality," *Economic History Review*, 29 (1968): 7–29.

3. Tacitus, *Annals*, bk. 1, chap. 8 (see Vignette 1.3, note 4).

4. Ibid., bk. 6 (year 33), p. 208.

5. Data from Tacitus's *Annals*.

6. Cassisu Dio, *The Roman History: The Reign of Augustus* (New York: Penguin Classics, 1987), 131.

7. From a personal communication.

8. Alfred Marshall, *Principles of Economics*, vol. 2: notes, 9th edition, Marshall's reply to criticism by William Cunningham (London: McMillan, 1961), 745.

9. This is five hundred times the GDP per capita of the United States (which in 2008 was about $42,000).

10. See Jessica Holzer, "Meet Senator Millionaire," *Forbes*, November 20, 2006, available at http://www.forbes.com/2006/11/17/senate-politics -washington-biz-wash_cx_jh_1120senate.html.

11. Milanovic, Lindert, and Williamson, "Preindustrial Inequality," appendix (see Vignette 1.3, note 5).

12. See ibid. and Walter Scheidel and Steven J. Friesen, "The Size of the Economy and the Distribution of Income in the Roman Empire," *Journal of Roman Studies* 99 (2009): 61–91. The Milanovic, Lindert, and Williamson estimate refers to the year 14, the Scheidel and Friesen to the year 150.

13. Maddison, *Contours of the World Economy*, 53–55 (see Vignette 1.3, note 5).

14. The richest region (peninsular Italy) was 50 percent above the mean, the poorest (the Danubian provinces) 25 percent below the mean.

15. For the definition of purchasing power parity (PPP) dollars, see Essay II.

Vignette 1.5

1. I am grateful to Vladimir Popov for very useful comments.

2. The practice started with Montek Ahluwalia, "Inequality, Poverty, and Development," *Journal of Development Economics* 3 (1976): 307–342.

3. See George Psacharopoulos and Harry Patrinos, *Returns to Investments in Education: A Further Update*, World Bank Policy Research Working Paper 2881 (Washington, DC: World Bank, September 2002).

4. This was particularly the case in the very egalitarian Czechoslovakia. The idea of demographic determination of income was introduced by Czech sociologist Jiři Večernik (see, e.g., *From Needs to the Market: Changing Inequality of Household Income in the Czech Transition*, William Davidson Institute Working Paper 370 [Ann Arbor: William Davidson Institute, April 2001]).

5. In the mid-1980s a Chinese friend living in Washington, DC, recounted to me that his ideological eye-opener came when, after volunteering to go as a Red Guard to a desolate area of Inner Mongolia, he read the state-commissioned and closely guarded translation of Djilas's *New Class*. The

chaos of the Cultural Revolution spread even to the special Communist Party libraries containing "secret books," and thus a young Maoist was transformed into a covert dissident.

6. A very nice historical discussion of this point can be found in Albert Hirschman's study *The Passions and the Interests* (Princeton: Princeton University Press, 1977), 127–128.

7. A famous case of being tried for parasitism was that of Joseph Brodsky, a Russian poet and later, after his exile to the United States, the Nobel laureate for literature.

Vignette 1.6

1. I am grateful to Guillaume Daudin for many excellent suggestions and comments that significantly improved the text, to Nathan Sussman for Parisian 13th-century data and map, and to Thomas Piketty for the data on 2007 fiscal incomes.

2. Actually, the Sixteenth is the second richest, just after the Seventh (but the Sixteenth has many more people).

3. The lowest income class includes families ("foyer fiscal") with incomes under €9,400 per year. The highest fiscal group is composed of families with annual incomes of €97,500 and above.

4. The analysis of the thirteenth-century data is based on Nathan Sussman's paper "Income Inequality in Paris in the Heyday of the Commercial Revolution" (unpublished MS).

5. See ibid., p. 3.

6. See http://www2.cnrs.fr/presse/thema/592.htm.

7. http://www.inshea.fr/RessourceProductions/SDADV/Tactimage_6e/Pages/PlanLutece.htm.

8. Emperor Julian, *The Mispogon*.

Vignette 1.7

1. The rationale is that the pension a person receives is, in principle, already paid for through wage deductions made during his working career, and thus is simply a wage income "restructured" in time. An exception are the so-called social pensions that are noncontributory and are paid to the poor elderly who, for example, have never worked (and thus have not earned a retirement income).

2. Branko Milanovic, "The Median Voter Hypothesis, Income Inequality, and Income Redistribution: An Empirical Test with the Required Data," *European Journal of Political Economy* 16, no. 3 (2000): 367–410.

Notes

Vignette 1.8

1. The position of Belarus is not clear. According to some statistics it is above, according to others just below, the Union-wide mean.

2. In addition to six republics I use the data for the two provinces (a lower administrative level than the republic).

Vignette 1.9

1. I am grateful to Vladimir Popov for his comments.

2. Although they are not all officially termed provinces, twenty-three are, and for simplicity I shall refer to all of them as "provinces."

3. All data come from the official Chinese sources, mostly from *China's Statistical Yearbook* (for various years).

4. Chongqing acquired the status of a separate unit (city-province) only in 1997.

5. Although one should not forget that the Baltic states were incorporated into czarist Russia beginning in the eighteenth century (broadly speaking, Estonia and Latvia since the end of the Swedish-Russian war in 1721, Lithuania after the partition of Poland in 1772).

Vignette 1.10

1. I am grateful to Peter Lindert for very useful comments and suggestions. See also Essay I on both Pareto's and Kuznets' theories of income distribution.

2. See Branko Milanovic, "Why We All Do Care About Inequality (but Are Loathe to Admit It)," *Challenge* 50, no. 6 (2007): 109–120.

3. David Kynaston, review of *Family Britain, 1951–57*, by Nicholas Spice, *London Review of Books*, April 8, 2010, 14.

4. It is somewhat extraordinary to realize that when Pareto was less than a year old, he lived within a kilometer of two illustrious neighbors: Karl Marx and his family, who, like the Paretos, lived nearby on the left bank, and Alexis de Tocqueville, then minister of foreign affairs, who lived near Place de la Madeleine on the right bank. For Pareto, born at 10 rue Guy-de-la Brosse, in the Fifth Arrondissement, see Pier Carlo Ferrera, "Appunti e precisazioni su alcuni aspetti della biografia di Vilfredo Pareto," *Paretiana*, no. 160. For Marx, living from June 3 to August 24, 1849, at 45 rue de Lille, in the Seventh Arrondissement, see Saul K. Padover, *Karl Marx: An Intimate Biography* (New York: Meridian, 1980), 359–360. For Tocqueville, see his *Souvenirs* (Paris: Gallimard, 1999), 239. I am grateful to Andrea Brandolini for the information on Pareto.

5. Raymond Aron, *Main Currents in Sociological Thought* (New York: Pelican, 1967), 2:176.

6. Vilfredo Pareto, *Manual of Political Economy*, translated by Ann S. Schwirr (New York: Augustus M. Kelley, 1971), 2.

7. "This is why Pareto will always remain apart among professors and sociologists. It is almost intolerable to the mind, at least to a teacher, to admit that truth in itself can be harmful" (Aron, *Main Currents*, 2:177).

8. Joseph Schumpeter, *A History of Economic Analysis* (1952; reprint, New York: Oxford University Press, 1980), 860.

9. The formula is a bit more complicated. Say that the "guillotine" is 1.45. If n people have incomes higher than y, then increasing the threshold to $1.1y$ would reduce the number of people with such high incomes to $n/(1.1)^{1.45} = n/1.148$.

10. Pareto, *Manual of Political Economy*, 312.

11. Pareto died in 1923, a year after Mussolini came to power in Italy. Some people have credited him with (or criticized him for) influence over Italian fascism, but the linkage, as Aron writes, is tenuous (*Main Currents*, 2:171–172).

12. See Peter H. Lindert, "Three Centuries of Inequality in Britain and the United States," in *Handbook of Income Distribution*, edited by Atkinson and Bourguignon (see Essay I, note 13); and Peter H. Lindert and Jeffrey G. Williamson, "Reinterpreting Britain's Social Tables, 1688–1913," *Explorations in Economic History* 20, no. 1 (1983): 94–109.

Essay II

1. *Mean income* and *GDP per capita* will be used interchangeably.

2. The numbers are even more striking if we compare the United States and India. The absolute gap in 1980 was less than $PPP 25,000; today it is more than $PPP 40,000.

3. In the previous period, 1990–2000, the gap was even wider (see Branko Milanovic, *Why Did the Poorest Countries Fail to Catch Up?* Carnegie Working Paper 62, (Washington, DC: Carnegie Endowment for International Peace, September 2005).

4. See also UNCTAD, *2007 World Investment Report* (Geneva: United Nations, 2007).

5. Robert Lucas, "Why Doesn't Capital Flow from Rich to Poor Countries?" *American Economic Review Papers and Proceeding* 80, no. 2 (1990): 92–96. The Lucas paradox also applies to labor: People with skills tend to migrate to countries where skills are abundant (the United States, Europe), not stay in their own skill-scarce countries.

6. Nicholas Crafts, *Globalization and Growth in the Twentieth Century*, IMF Working Paper 2000/44 (Washington, DC: International Monetary

Fund, March 2000), 26–27, 30. See also Richard Baldwin and Philippe Martin, *Two Waves of Globalisation: Superficial Similarities, Fundamental Differences*, National Bureau of Economic Research Working Paper 6904 (Cambridge, MA: National Bureau of Economic Research, January 1999).

7. Data from Maurice Obsfeld and Alan Taylor, "Globalization and Capital Markets," in *Globalization in Historical Perspective*, edited by Michael D. Bordo, Alan M. Taylor, and Jeffrey G. Williamson (Chicago: University of Chicago Press, 2003), 121–187, quoted in Niall Ferguson and Moritz Schularick, "The Empire Effect: The Determinants of Country Risk in the First Age of Globalization, 1880–1913," *Journal of Economic History* (June 2006): 285.

8. Paul Romer, "The Origins of Endogenous Growth," *Journal of Economic Perspectives* 8, no. 1 (1994): 3–22.

9. Paul Romer, "Are Non-convexities Important for Understanding Growth?" *American Economic Review* [Papers and Proceedings of the American Economic Association] 80, no. 2 (1990): 97–103.

Vignette 2.1

1. See Peter H. Lindert and Jeffrey G. Williamson, "Revising England's Social Tables, 1688–1812," *Explorations in Economic History* 19, no. 4 (1982): 385–408; Lindert and Williamson, "Reinterpreting Britain's Social Tables" (see Vignette 1.10, note 13); and Lindert, "Three Centuries of Inequality" (see Vignette 1.10, note 13).

2. See Jan Luiten van Zanden, "Tracing the Beginning of the Kuznets Curve: Western Europe During the Early Modern Period," *Economic History Review* 48, no. 4 (1995): 643–664. For Germany, see Rolf Dumke, "Income Inequality and Industrialization in Germany, 1850–1913: The Kuznets Hypothesis Revisited," in *Income Distribution in Historical Perspective*, edited by Y. S. Brenner, Harmut Kaeble, and Mark Thomas (Cambridge: Cambridge University Press, 1991).

3. Based on Angus Maddison's data. For the early nineteenth century, Belgian-Swiss economic historian Paul Bairoch gives an even smaller gap, around 2 to 1, between the richest and poorest nations (*Victoires et déboires: Histoire économique et sociale du monde du XVIe siècle à nos jours* [Paris: Gallimard, 1997], 1:111). Today the gap between the Netherlands and China, despite China's phenomenal growth over the past quarter century, is 8 to 1. Or take the following example: Around 1760, the gap between Great Britain and India was less than 1.5 to 1 (Bairoch, 2:845). Today, it is 13 to 1.

4. Gregory Clark, "The Condition of the Working Class in England, 1209–2004," *Journal of Political Economy* 115, no. 6 (2005): 1307–1340.

5. In a letter to Marx in 1858: "The English proletariat is actually becoming more and more bourgeois. . . . For a nation which exploits the whole world this is of course to a certain extent justifiable" (*Marx and Engels: Selected Correspondence*, 4th ed. [Moscow: Progress, 1982], 132). See also Eric Hobsbawm, *The Age of Capital* (New York: Vintage Books, 1996) (in particular, 224–229).

6. Leon Trotsky, *Le terrorisme et communisme* (Paris: Edition 10/18, 1963) (originally published in Russian in 1920).

7. "Permanent revolution" is Trotsky's and Lenin's idea that the proletarian revolution, having been successful in the relatively backward Russia, must soon break out in the more developed parts of the world, thus fulfilling Marx's own expectations and instituting communism worldwide.

8. Solidarity based on religion is an altogether different matter.

Vignette 2.4

1. In 2006 it was estimated that there were 191 million people (3 percent of the world population) living in countries where they were not born (Richard Freeman, *People Flows in Globalization*, National Bureau of Economic Research Working Paper 12315 [Cambridge, MA: National Bureau of Economic Research, 2006]). Note that this is a stock, that is, the "accumulation" of all such people through the years. The flows (annual increases in such a stock) are of course much smaller: around 3 million people annually (see http://www.oecd.org/dataoecd/17/39/23664717.gif).

2. In 2008, 15.6 percent of the U.S. labor force was foreign born (see Bureau of Labor Statistics, *News Release*, March 26, 2009, at http://www.bls.gov/cps/). For Spain, see Instituto Nacional de Estatistica, *Labor Force Survey* (Madrid: Instituto Nacional de Estatistica, 2008). For Greece, see *Employment in OECD Countries* (year 2002), available at http://www.childpolicyintl.org/contexttablesemployment/Table%202.31%20Employment%20in%20OECD%20countries.pdf. For Italy, see Banca d'Italia, *Relazione annuale sul 2008*, May 29, 2009, chap. 11, table 11.4, p. 128, available at http://www.bancaditalia.it/pubblicazioni/relann/rel08/rel08it/.

3. See David Blanchflower and Chris Shadforth, "Fear, Unemployment, and Migration," *Economic Journal* (February 2009): table 17, p. F157.

4. U.S. Department of Homeland Security, based on the estimated increase in Mexican illegal immigrants between 2000 and 2005 (1.3 million).

5. The total number of people killed while trying to cross the Berlin Wall was around two hundred during its twenty-seven-year existence. On an annual basis, the number of Mexican deaths is thus fifty *times* greater.

6. BBC, July 2, 2007, http://news.bbc.co.uk/2/hi/europe/6228236.stm.

Vignette 2.5

1. Several hundred Algerian and Tunisian nationals are thought to be imprisoned in Libyan jails.

2. BBC, March 31, 2009; Radio France Inter, March 16, 2009.

3. Ironically, one may recall that in the nineteenth century many Maltese, Sicilians, and Corsicans freely moved over and settled in Tunisia.

4. The Algerian daily *El Watan*, March 5, 2009.

5. Agence France Presse, March 31, 2009.

Vignette 2.6

1. The grandfather was born in 1895 (died in 1979), the father was born in 1936 (died in 1982), BHO was born in 1961. Onyango's first child (Sarah) was born in 1933 when he was thirty-eight, a rather advanced age to have a first child in the Kenya of the 1930s.

2. Barack Obama, *Dreams from My Father* (New York: Crown, 2007), 426.

3. Assuming no holidays, no absence due to sickness, and so forth.

4. Onyango's family will eventually include himself, two wives, and five children.

5. Arne Bigston, *Income Distribution and Growth in a Dual Economy: Kenya, 1914–1976*, Memorandum 101 (Gothenburg: Gothenburg University, Department of Economics, 1987).

6. Barack Obama, *Dreams from My Father*, 47.

Vignette 2.7

1. I am grateful to Vladimir Popov and Michael Ellman for help with Soviet growth data.

2. Angus Maddison's 2004 population and GDP per capita data are used throughout this vignette (unless when explicitly mentioned otherwise).

3. The latter figure is based on Mark Harrison, *The Economics of World War II: Six Great Powers in International Comparison* (Cambridge: Cambridge University Press, 1998), 95.

Essay III

1. Karl Marx, *A Contribution to the Critique of Political Economy* (preface).

2. See Branko Milanovic, *Worlds Apart: Measuring International and Global Inequality* (Princeton: Princeton University Press, 2005). The reason we have to use benchmark years is because household surveys are not available annu-

ally for all countries. We need to open a relatively large "window" of five years within which surveys for practically all countries in the world are available, then "fix" one year among these five, and for countries that lack surveys for that particular year use surveys from the "neighboring years."

3. This is calculated using the most recent PPP data from 2005 (see Essay II for details).

4. In the key work on the historical pattern of global inequality (reviewed below) Bourguignon and Morrisson lack, of course, any estimate of income distributions for most countries of the world. They divide the world into thirty-three regions and to all countries within a region ascribe the same distribution that they have for one country of the region. It leads, of course, to some gross, and wrong, generalizations whereby, for example, income distributions existing in the countries with very unequal landholdings (as in czarist Russia) are ascribed to the countries in the Balkans, characterized, on the contrary, by peasant-owned small plots of land. But, due to the lack of data, one cannot do any better than that.

5. François Bourguignon and Christian Morrisson, "The Size Distribution of Income Among World Citizens, 1820–1990," *American Economic Review* (September 2002): 727–744 (see table on 731–732).

6. See Glenn Firebaugh, *The New Geography of Global Income Inequality* (Cambridge: Harvard University Press, 2003); and Robert Lucas, "The Industrial Revolution: Past and Future" (mimeograph, University of Chicago, 1998).

7. See Branko Milanovic, "True World Income Distribution, 1988 and 1993: First Calculations Based on Household Surveys Alone," *Economic Journal* 112, no. 476 (2002): 81.

8. Jagdish Bhagwati, *In Defense of Globalization* (Oxford: Oxford University Press, 2004), 67.

9. Thomas Nagel, "The Problem of Global Justice," *Philosophy and Public Affairs* 33, no. 2 (2005): 121.

10. See Charles Beitz, *Political Theory and International Relations* (1977; reprint, Princeton: Princeton University Press, 1999), 164–169.

11. See Charles Beitz, "Rawls' Law of Peoples," *Ethics* 110, no. 4 (2000): 669–696; and Joshua Cohen and Charles Sabel, "Extra Rempublicam Nulla Justitia," *Philosophy and Public Affairs* 34, no. 2 (2005).

12. This is called "monism": All ethically meaningful relationships are between individuals (not mediated by the state), and there are no different "circles of affinity" such that we would give more weight to the economic deprivation of our family members or compatriots than to the poverty of

people whom we may not even know personally (see, for example, Thomas Pogge, "An Egalitarian Law of Peoples," *Philosophy and Public Affairs* 23, no. 3 [1994]: 195–224; and Peter Singer, *One World: The Ethics of Globalization* [New Haven: Yale University Press, 2002]).

Vignette 3.1

1. If capital gains are "too high," statisticians generally round them off to a high but lower number (a "ceiling"). This is called "top coding." In the United States, top coding of interest, dividends, and other property income can, it is argued, seriously reduce measured inequality (see Burkhauser et al., *Estimating Trends in U.S. Income Inequality* [see Essay I, note 27]).

2. The number of household members may sometimes be, say, three and a half if your child lived with you half a year.

3. I do not expect people whose income is less than the world median to buy my book—a sad but probable state of affairs. The cost of this book is around twenty-five dollars. People whose income is less than the world median would have to spend one-quarter of their monthly income on the book. Would you do it? Would I?

4. The total number of people included in 2005 surveys is just under 6 billion. About 5 percent of people in the world, living in the poorest and most conflict-ridden countries such as Sudan, Afghanistan, North Korea, Somalia, and Iraq, are not included since their countries do not conduct national household surveys. Thus, all inequality results shown here are (slight) underestimates compared to "real" values.

5. It takes $90,000 of net income per capita to be in the top 1 percent of U.S. income distribution.

6. We know that $60/(2.06)^\alpha$ has to yield 6. Hence, $\alpha = 3.2$.

Vignette 3.2

1. One example is Thomas Friedman, *The World Is Flat* (New York: Farrar, Straus, and Giroux, 2005).

2. Pioneered by Lester Thurow, "A Surge in Inequality," *Scientific American* 256 (1987), it was used recently in Carol Graham, Nancy Birdsall, and Stefano Pettinato, *Stuck in the Tunnel: Is Globalization Muddling the Middle?* Brookings Institution Center Working Paper 14 (Washington, DC: Brookings Institution, August 2000); and Steven Pressman, "The Decline of the Middle Class: An International Perspective," *Journal of Economic Issues* 40, no. 1 (2007): 181–200, in a study of the middle class in eleven developed countries. In income distributions, the mean income is typically higher than

the median because income distributions are not symmetrical: The bottom is cut off (one cannot survive on zero income), while the top income extends to very high (almost unlimited) amounts.

3. These values allow us also to calculate what percentage of total income is received by the middle class. In Latin America it is only 12 percent (20 percent of the population times 0.6 of mean incomes) and in advanced economies 34 percent (40 percent of the population times 0.85 of mean incomes).

4. It may be a matter of disagreement whether the classification of Turkey as part of the Western world is appropriate. However, its candidate status for the European Union, as well as the fact that it is not a postcommunist country, makes its classification as part of the West (together with Israel) reasonable.

5. Abhijit Banerjee and Esther Duflo, "What Is Middle About Middle Classes Around the World," *Journal of Economic Perspectives* 22, no. 2 (2008): 3–28, based on a sample of thirteen developing countries.

6. Cell phones are sociologically very interesting. Because of their relatively low cost and the lack of very manifest differentiation among models, they have become social equalizers. It is odd that they still convey the feeling of exclusiveness, but I believe that it is due to the "message" of connectivity that they project. I remember seeing teenagers in Tashkent, Uzbekistan, in the early 2000s who carried tucked in their belts empty shells of cell phones (which did not work but just looked impressive).

Vignette 3.3

1. The dispersal of GDPs per capita by state, shown in the map on page 179 for consistency with the European Union, is just slightly wider: a top-to-bottom ratio of two to one.

2. See Rati Ram, "Interstate Income Inequality in the United States: Measurement, Modelling, and Some Characteristics," *Review of Income and Wealth* 38 (1992): 39–49.

Vignette 3.4

1. Latin America is defined to include South America and Central America (Spanish-speaking countries plus Brazil and Guyana), not the Caribbean. The poorest country in the Western Hemisphere is Haiti. For Asia, we lack the data for North Korea (which is very poor) and do not include the oil-rich western Asia (Middle Eastern) countries.

2. The latter one being, of course, part of China.

Vignette 3.5

1. I am grateful to Georgie Milanovic for his comments.

2. In a recent high-level match Liverpool demolished the iconic Spanish side of Real Madrid by 4–0. But the same number of Spaniards played on both teams—four—and in addition the all too important coach of Liverpool was Spanish. So, yes, the Spanish icon lost, but strangely it lost (mostly) at the hands, or rather the feet, of Spaniards!

3. The first two championships were invitational. After that, clubs had to qualify either by winning the previous European championship or by being highly placed in national leagues.

4. The 2008 list of the twenty richest European clubs was made by Deloitte Sports Business Group (published in February 2009). For the list, see http://www.theoffside.com/world-football/the-20-richest-teams-in-the-world-in-2008.html.

5. Although many soccer fans would argue the reverse: that it is life that imitates soccer.

Vignette 3.6

1. A substantially same text was published on the Web by Yale Global online (May 4, 2009). I am grateful for the authorization to reproduce it here.

2. See Thomas Piketty and Emmanuel Saez, "Income Inequality in the United States, 1913–2002," fig. 2, May 2005 version, available at http://elsa.berkeley.edu/~saez/piketty-saezOUP05US.pdf.

3. Thomas Piketty and Emmanuel Saez (2006), "The evolution of top incomes: a historical and international perspective," *American Economic Review*, vol. 96, no. 2, 2006, p. 200–205.

4. Charles de Montesquieu, *Lettres persanes*, letter 142.

Vignette 3.7

1. Based on joint work with Peter Lindert and Jeffrey Williamson.

2. Defined by Branko Milanovic, "An Estimate of Average Income and Inequality in Byzantium Around Year 1000," *Review of Income and Wealth* 52, no. 3 (2006): 449–470; and Milanovic, Lindert, and Williamson, *Measuring Ancient Inequality* (see Vignette 1.3, note 5).

3. There are also two Ottoman colonies in the sample (South Serbia in 1455 and Levant in 1596), but their data do not include the estimated incomes of the colonizers.

4. In approximately today's PPP dollars.

5. British income distribution data for 2004.

Vignette 3.8

1. John Rawls, *The Law of Peoples* (Cambridge: Harvard University Press, 1999), 39.

2. "Peoples have a duty to assist other peoples living under unfavorable conditions that prevent their having a just or decent political and social regime" (ibid., 37).

3. Ibid., 114. Liberal and decent societies are the two kinds of "well-ordered peoples." Roughly speaking, liberal societies are fully democratic, while decent societies may be "consultative hierarchical societies." However, both societies respect each other's choices and are willing to live in peace.

4. Ibid., 144.

5. Joshua Cohen, "Comments on Rodrik" (unpublished MS), 5.

Vignette 3.9

1. For example, Argentina, by virtue of being in Latin America, was seemingly part of the third world. Yet most people there saw themselves as an extension of Europe.

2. The data are expressed in 2005 PPP dollars.

3. Argentina at $PPP 10,000 was richer, but we have noted the ambivalence of Argentina's position. Venezuela too was richer but mostly thanks to oil.

4. This quote predates *Wealth of Nations* by some ten years, which makes Smith's prescience even more remarkable.

5. The strange thing is that both proponents of more aid for Africa and those who are against all aid blame the West, the first for not helping enough, the latter for helping too much. Is there an optimal aid amount?

6. See Giovanni Arrighi, "The African Crisis: World Systemic and Regional Aspects," *New Left Review* (May–June 2002).

7. The first stanza of the poem, "The Wise Perceive Imminent Events," was written between 1905 and 1915. The poem has as its epigram the sentence from Philostratus, the third century Greek writer: "The gods perceive future events, mortals present ones, and the wise perceive what is imminent." (Constantine Cavafy, *Selected Poems* (New York: Penguin Classics, 2008); translated by Avi Sharon, p. 27).

Further Readings

Essay I

Seminal Texts

Kuznets, Simon. "Economic Growth and Income Inequality." Presidential address delivered to the sixty-seventh meeting of the American Economic Association, Michigan, December 1954. Published in *American Economic Review* 45, no. 1 (March 1955). [First description of the famous inverted U inequality curve.]

———. *Economic Growth and Structure: Selected Essays.* New Delhi: Oxford University Press and IBH, 1965. [Selected papers on inequality, industrial structure, and demography.]

Pareto, Vilfredo. *Manual of Political Economy.* Translated by Ann S. Schwirr. 1906. Reprint, New York: Augustus M. Kelley, 1971. [Pareto's economics textbook, and much more.]

———. "On the Distribution of Wealth and Income." *Rivista di Politica Economica* (August–September 1997): 645–660. Originally published as *La courbe de la répartition de la richesse.* Lausanne: Université de Lausanne, 1896. [Formulation of Pareto's regularities of income distribution and definition of Pareto's constant.]

Rawls, John. *A Theory of Justice.* Cambridge: Harvard University Press, 1971. [Formulation of "justice as fairness" theory; the difference principle.]

Kuznets' Hypothesis and Its Extensions

Anand, Sudhir, and Ravi Kanbur. "The Kuznets Process and the Inequality-Development Relationship." *Journal of Development Economics* (1993): 25–52. [A detailed test of Kuznets' hypothesis.]

Li, Hongyi, Lyn Squire, and Heng-fou Zou. "Explaining International and Intertemporal Variations in Income Inequality." *Economic Journal* 108 (1998): 26–43. [Rejection of Kuznets' hypothesis based on relative fixity of country Ginis over time.]

Milanovic, Branko. *Determinants of Cross-country Income Inequality: An "Augmented" Kuznets' Hypothesis.* World Bank Policy Research Paper 1246. Washington, DC: World Bank, 1994. [Kuznets' hypothesis holds if we adjust it for government spending and state-sector employment share.]

Snowdon, Brian. "Towards a Unified Theory of Economic Growth: Oded Galor on the Transition from Malthusian Stagnation to Modern Economic Growth." *World Economics* 9, no. 2 (2008): 97–151. [Why the importance of "being equal" changes in the course of economic development.]

Inequality in the Last Century

Atkinson, Anthony B. "The Distribution of Income in the UK and OECD Countries in the Twentieth Century." *Oxford Review of Economic Policy* 15, no. 4 (1999): 56–75. [A broad overview of rich countries' inequality.]

Atkinson, Anthony B., and John Micklewright. *Economic Transformation in Eastern Europe and the Distribution of Income.* Cambridge: Cambridge University Press, 1992. [An excellent introduction to the principles that guided income distribution under socialism and to the actual inequality outcomes, covering the period from the 1960s to the fall of socialism.]

Brandolini, Andrea, and Tim M. Smeeding. "Inequality Patterns in Western Democracies: Cross-country Differences and Changes over Time." In *Democracy, Inequality, and Representation: A Comparative Perspective,* edited by Paolo Beramandi and Christopher J. Anderson. New York: Russell Sage Foundation, 2008. [Excellent overview of inequality changes in the past fifty years, country by country.]

Deaton, Angus, and Jean Dreze. "Poverty and Inequality in India: A Reexamination." *Economic and Political Weekly* (September 7, 2002): 3729–3748.

Fields, Gary. *Distribution and Development: A New Look at the Developing World.* Cambridge: MIT Press, 2001. [An excellent review of income inequality and income mobility in developing countries.]

Gasparini, Leonardo, Guillermo Cruces, Leopoldo Tornarolli, and Mariana Marchionni. "A Turning Point? Recent Developments on Inequality in Latin America and the Caribbean." *Economia* (2010). Available also at http://cedias.econo.unlp.edu.ar/eng/working=papers.php. [Reviews inequality and polarization in Latin America and the Caribbean over the past thirty years.]

Milanovic, Branko. *Income, Inequality, and Poverty During the Transition from Planned to Market Economy.* Washington, DC: World Bank, 1998. [The effects of transition on income inequality in postcommunist countries.]

Organization for Economic Cooperation and Development. *Growing Unequal? Income Distribution and Poverty in OECD Countries.* Paris: OECD, October 2008. [Two decades of increased inequality in the rich world.]

Piketty, Thomas. "Income Inequality in France, 1901–1998." *Journal of Political Economy* 111, no. 5 (2003): 1004–1042. [Original study introducing Piketty's methodology and hypotheses, based on an earlier book published in French.]

———. "Top Income Shares in the Long Run: An Overview." *Journal of European Economic Association* 3, nos. 2–3 (2005): 1–11. [An overview of inequality in advanced economies in the twentieth century.]

Piketty, Thomas, and Emmanuel Saez. "Income Inequality in the United States, 1913–1998." *Quarterly Journal of Economics* 118, no. 1 (2003): 1–39. [The same as the study of France but now applied to U.S. data.]

Ravallion, Martin, and Shaohua Chen. "China's (Uneven) Progress Against Poverty." *Journal of Development Economics* 82 (2006): 1–42. [Inequality and poverty in China since the reforms in the early 1980s.]

How Inequality Affects Other Economic Variables

Alesina, Alberto, and Roberto Perotti. "The Political Economy of Growth: A Critical Survey of the Recent Literature." *World Bank Economic Review*, no. 8 (1994): 350–371. [Discussion of the median-voter hypothesis.]

Barro, Robert. "Inequality and Growth in a Panel of Countries." *Journal of Economic Growth* (March 2000): 5–32. [A massive exercise although with often dubious data.]

Lundberg, Mattias, and Lyn Squire. "The Simultaneous Evolution of Growth and Inequality." *Economic Journal* 113 (April 2003): 326–344. [Can policy makers target both growth and inequality?]

Perotti, Roberto. "Growth, Income Distribution, and Democracy: What the Data Say." *Journal of Economic Growth* 1 (1996): 149–187. [The link among the three key variables listed in the title explored empirically.]

Rogowski, Ron. "What Changes Inequality and What Does Inequality Change?" Unpublished MS, December 2008, available at http://www.sscnet.ucla.edu/polisci/cpworkshop/papers/Rogowski.pdf. [Different ways inequality influences other variables and they influence inequality, with more of a sociological perspective.]

Thorbecke, Erik, and Chutatong Charumilind. "Economic Inequality and Its Socioeconomic Impact." *World Development* 30, no. 2 (2002): 1477–1495. [Reviews all channels of influence of inequality on other economic variables.]

Vignette 1.1

Allen, Robert C. *Capital Accumulation, Technological Change, and the Distribution of Income During the British Industrial Revolution.* Department of Economics Discussion Paper 239. Oxford: Oxford University, June 2005.

Lindert, Peter H. "Three Centuries of Inequality in Britain and the United States." In *Handbook of Income Distribution*, edited by A. Atkinson and F. Bourguignon. Amsterdam: Elvesier, 2000.

Lindert, Peter H., and Jeffrey G. Williamson. "Reinterpreting Britain's Social Tables, 1688–1913." *Explorations in Economic History* 20, no. 1 (1983): 94–109.

Vignette 1.3

Baker, Peter, and Susan Glasser. *Kremlin Rising: Vladimir Putin's Russia and the End of Revolution.* New York: Scribner's, 2005. [See especially chapter 14.]

Chernov, Ron. *Titan: The Life of John D. Rockefeller.* New York: Vintage Books, 1998.

Freeland, Chrystia. *Sale of the Century: Russia's Wild Ride from Communism to Capitalism.* New York: Random House, 2000.

Nasaw, David. *Andrew Carnegie.* New York: Penguin, 2006.

Wright, Lawrence. "Slim's Time." *New Yorker,* June 1, 2009, 58.

Vignette 1.4

Goldsmith, Raymond W. "An Estimate of the Size and Structure of the National Product of the Early Roman Empire." *Review of Income and Wealth* 30, no. 3 (September 1984): 263–288.

Maddison, Angus. *Contours of the World Economy, 1–2030 AD.* Oxford: Oxford University Press, 2007.

Milanovic, Branko. *New Palgrave Dictionary of Economics*, edited by Steven N. Durlauf and Laurence E. Blume, s.v. "Preindustrial Inequality." Palgrave: McMillan, 2009.

Milanovic, Branko, Peter H. Lindert, and Jeffrey G. Williamson. "Preindustrial Inequality." *Economic Journal*, forthcoming. Previous version published as *Measuring Ancient Inequality.* National Bureau of Economic Research Working Paper 13550. Cambridge, MA: National Bureau of Economic Research, 2009.

Scheidel, Walter, and Steven J. Friesen. "The Size of the Economy and the Distribution of Income in the Roman Empire." *Journal of Roman Studies* 99 (2009): 61–91.

Schiavone, Aldo. *The End of the Past: Ancient Rome and the Modern West.* Cambridge: Harvard University Press, 2000.

Tacitus, Cornelius. *The Annals.* New York: Penguin, 1996.

Vignette 1.5

Atkinson, Anthony B., and John Micklewright. *Economic Transformation in Eastern Europe and the Distribution of Income.* Cambridge: Cambridge University Press, 1992.

Bergson, Abram. "Income Inequality Under Soviet Socialism." *Journal of Economic Literature* 22, no. 3 (1984): 1052–1099.

Brown, Henry Phelps. *Egalitarianism and the Generation of Inequality.* Oxford: Clarendon Press, 1998. [See especially chapter 10.]

Djilas, Milovan. *The New Class: An Analysis of the Communist System.* 1957. Reprint, New York: Harvest and Harcourt Brace Jovanovich.

Goldman, Emma. *My Disillusionment in Russia (1919–21).* 1923. Reprint, Mineola, NY: Dover.

Milanovic, Branko. *Income, Inequality, and Poverty During the Transition from Planned to Market Economy.* Washington, DC: World Bank, 1998.

Redor, Dominique. *Wage Inequalities in East and West.* Cambridge: Cambridge University Press, 1992. [First published in French in 1988.]

Trotsky, Lev. *The Revolution Betrayed.* 1936. Reprint, Mineola, NY: Dover.

Yanowitch, Murray. *Social and Economic Inequality in the Soviet Union.* White Plains, NY: M. E. Sharpe, 1977.

Vignette 1.7

Bassett, William, John Burkett, and Louis Putterman. "Income Distribution, Government Transfers, and the Problem of Unequal Influence." *European Journal of Political Economy* 15 (1999): 207–228.

Mahler, Vincent. *Electoral Turnout and Income Redistribution by the State: A Cross-national Analysis of Developed Democracies.* Luxembourg Income Study Working Paper 455. Luxembourg: Luxembourg Income Study, December 2006.

Meltzer, Allan H., and Scott Richard. "A Rational Theory of the Size of Government." *Journal of Political Economy* 89, no. 5 (1981): 914–927.

Milanovic, Branko. "The Median Voter Hypothesis, Income Inequality, and Income Redistribution: An Empirical Test with the Required Data." *European Journal of Political Economy* 16, no. 3 (2000): 367–410.

Scervini, Francesco. "The Empirics of the Median Voter: Democracy, Redistribution, and the Role of the Middle Class." *Scandinavian Journal of Economics*. Forthcoming.

Vignette 1.9

Amalrik, Andrei. *L'Union soviétique survivra-t-elle en 1984?* Paris: Pluriel, 1977.

Aroca, Patricio A., Dong Guo, and Geoffrey J. D. Hewings. "Spatial Convergence in China, 1952–99." In *Inequality and Growth in Modern China*, edited by Gunghua Wan, 125–143. UNU-WIDER Studies in Development Economics. Oxford: Oxford University Press, 2008.

Kanbur, Ravi, and Xiaobo Zhang. "Fifty Years of Regional Inequality in China: A Journey Through Central Planning, Reform, and Openness." *Review of Development Economics* 9, no. 1 (2005): 87–106.

Lin, Justin Yifu, and Peilin Liu. "Development Strategies and Regional Income Disparities in China." In *Inequality and Growth in Modern China*, edited by Gunghua Wan, 56–78. UNU-WIDER Studies in Development Economics. Oxford: Oxford University Press, 2008.

Milanovic, Branko. "Half a World: Regional Inequality in Five Great Federations." *Journal of Asia Pacific Economy* 10, no. 4 (2005): 408–445.

Popov, Vladimir. "China's Rise, Russia's Fall: Medium-Term and Long-Term Perspective." Paper presented at the Global Development Conference, Beijing, January 2007.

Ravallion, Martin, and Shaohua Chen. "China's (Uneven) Progress Against Poverty." *Journal of Development Economics* 82, no. 1 (2007): 1–42.

Vignette 1.10

Aron, Raymond. *Main Currents in Sociological Thought*. Vol. 2. New York: Pelican, 1967. [Overview of sociological contributions of Durkheim, Pareto, and Weber.]

Creedy, John. *Dynamics of Income Distribution*. New York: Basil Blackwell, 1985. [Includes a detailed discussion of Pareto's papers and findings.]

Fogel, Robert W. *Simon S. Kuznets, April 30, 1901–July 2, 1985*. National Bureau of Economic Research Working Paper 7787. Cambridge, MA:

National Bureau of Economic Research, July 2000. [An "accountant-style" biography of Kuznets.]

Kuznets, Simon. "Economic Growth and Income Inequality." Presidential address delivered to the sixty-seventh meeting of the American Economic Association, Michigan, December 1954. Published in *American Economic Review* 45, no. 1 (March 1955). [First description of the famous inverted U inequality curve.]

———. *Economic Growth and Structure: Selected Essays.* New Delhi: Oxford University Press and IBH, 1965. [Selected papers on inequality, industrial structure, and demography.]

Pareto, Vilfredo. *Manual of Political Economy.* Translated by Ann S. Schwirr. 1906. Reprint, New York: Augustus M. Kelley, 1971. [Pareto's economics textbook, and much more.]

———. "On the Distribution of Wealth and Income." *Rivista di Politica Economica* (August–September 1997): 645–660. Originally published as *La courbe de la répartition de la richesse.* Lausanne: Université de Lausanne, 1896. [Formulation of Pareto's regularities of income distribution and definition of Pareto's constant. The same issue of *Rivista di Politica Economica* contains English translations of five other articles by Pareto on the topic of income distribution.]

Schumpeter, Joseph A. *History of Economic Analysis.* 1952. Reprint, New York: Oxford University Press, 1980. [Perhaps the best, and surely the most erudite, history of economic thought.]

Essay II

Books

Bairoch, Paul. *Victoires et déboires: Histoire économique et sociale du monde du XVIe siècle à nos jours.* 3 vols. Paris: Gallimard, 1997. [A magisterial three-volume book on economic history from the conquest of the Americas to Gorbachev; in urgent need of English translation. See especially volume 3, part 5.]

Collier, Paul. *The Bottom Billion.* Oxford: Oxford University Press, 2007. [Why Africa is poor.]

Maddison, Angus. *Contours of the World Economy, 1–2030 AD.* Oxford: Oxford University Press, 2007. [Economic growth of nations over the past two centuries—and even beyond—quantified and explained.]

Milanovic, Branko. *Worlds Apart: Measuring International and Global Inequality.* Princeton: Princeton University Press, 2005. [Introduction of three concepts of global inequality and analysis of their evolution since 1950.]

Further Readings

Articles

DeLong, Brandford, and Steve Dowrick. "Globalization and Convergence." Chapter 4 in *Globalization in Historical Perspective*, edited by M. Bordo, A. M. Taylor, and J. Williamson. Chicago: Chicago University Press, 2003. [The puzzle of missing income convergence among countries during Globalization 2.0.]

Grier, Kevin, and Robin Grier. "Only Income Diverges: A Neoclassical Anomaly." *Journal of Development Economics* 84 (2007): 25–45. [Why everything converges, as we would expect, but incomes do not.]

Milanovic, Branko. *Where in the World Are You? Assessing the Importance of Circumstance and Effort in a World of Different Mean Country Incomes and (Almost) No Migration.* World Bank Working Paper 4493. Washington, DC: World Bank, January 2008. [Inequality of country mean incomes implies inequality in individual opportunities.]

Minoiu, Camelia, and Sanjay Reddy. "Real Income Stagnation of Countries, 1960–2001." *Journal of Development Studies* 45, no. 1 (2009): 1–23. [How and why many poor and middle-income countries failed to catch up.]

Pritchett, Lant. "Divergence, Big Time." *Journal of Economic Perspectives* 11, no. 3 (1997): 3–17. [Do not think of convergence among the small subset of rich countries when the world is diverging!]

Quah, Danny. "Empirics for Economic Growth and Convergence: Stratification and Convergence Clubs." *European Economic Review* 40 (1996): 427–443. [First formulation of "twin peaks"—a rich and a poor peak—of international income distribution.]

Romer, Paul. "The Origins of Endogenous Growth." *Journal of Economic Perspectives* 8, no. 1 (1994): 3–22. [Explains how the new approach to growth evolved in response to real-world departures from mainstream neoclassical theory.]

Vignette 2.1

Bairoch, Paul. *Economics and World History: Myths and Paradoxes.* Chicago: University of Chicago Press, 1993.

———. *Victoires et déboires: Histoire économique et sociale du monde du XVIe siècle à nos jours.* Paris: Gallimard, 1997. [A magisterial three-volume book on economic history from the conquest of the Americas to Gorbachev; in urgent need of English translation.]

Bourguignon, François, and Christian Morrisson. "The Size Distribution of Income Among World Citizens, 1820–1990." *American Economic Review* (September 2002): 727–744. [First empirical study of global inequality in its historical context.]

Hobsbawm, Eric. *The Age of Capital, 1848–1875*. 1975. Reprint, New York: Vintage Books, 1996. [A brilliant "haute vulgarisation," as Hobsbawm calls it; second part of the tetralogy, which starts with "The Age of Revolution, 1789–1848."]

———. *The Age of Empire, 1875–1914*. New York: Vintage Books, 1987. [Sequel to the previous volume.]

Maddison, Angus. *The World Economy: Historical Statistics*. Paris: OECD Development Centre Studies, 2003. [Indispensable historical statistics.]

———. *The World Economy: A Millennial Perspective*. Paris: OECD Development Centre Studies, 2001. [A brilliant sketch of global economic history and the only source of historical data on GDPs for more than one hundred countries.]

Marx, Karl. *The Communist Manifesto*. [Locus classicum.]

Milanovic, Branko. *Worlds Apart: Measuring International and Global Inequality*. Princeton: Princeton University Press, 2005. [Introduction of three concepts of global inequality and analysis of their evolution since 1950.]

Vignette 2.2

Freeman, Richard. *People Flows in Globalization*. National Bureau of Economic Research Working Paper 12315. Cambridge, MA: National Bureau of Economic Research, 2006.

Milanovic, Branko. "Rules of Redistribution and Foreign Aid: A Proposal for a Change in the Rules Governing Eligibility for Foreign Aid." *Interventions* 5, no. 1 (2008): 197–214.

———. *Worlds Apart: Measuring International and Global Inequality*. Princeton: Princeton University Press, 2005.

Vignette 2.3

Milanovic, Branko. *Global Inequality of Opportunity*. World Bank Working Paper 4493. Washington, DC: World Bank, January 2008.

Shachar, Ayelet. *The Birthright Lottery: Citizenship and Global Inequality*. Cambridge: Harvard University Press, 2009.

Vignette 2.7

Bairoch, Paul. *Victoires et déboires: Histoire économique et sociale du monde du XVIe siècle à nos jours*. 3 vols. Paris: Gallimard, 1997. [See especially volume 3, chapter 24.]

Crafts, Nicholas. *Globalization and Growth in the Twentieth Century*. IMF Working Paper 2000/44. Washington, DC: International Monetary Fund, March 2000.

Harrison, Mark. *The Economics of World War II: Six Great Powers in International Comparison*. Cambridge: Cambridge University Press, 1998.

Lewis, Arthur. *Economic Survey, 1919–1939*. London: George Allen and Unwin, 1949.

Milanovic, Branko. "Economic Integration and Income Convergence: Not Such a Strong Link?" *Review of Economics and Statistics* 88, no. 4 (2006): 659–670.

Essay III

Books

Firebaugh, Glenn. *The New Geography of Global Income Inequality*. Cambridge: Harvard University Press, 2003. [Overview of inequalities among countries with some rough estimates of global inequality among people in the world.]

Milanovic, Branko. *Worlds Apart: Measuring International and Global Inequality*. Princeton: Princeton University Press, 2005. [Global inequality calculations, based on household surveys, from 1988 to 2002.]

Pogge, Thomas, and Darrel Moellendorf. *Global Justice: Seminal Essays*. Paragon Issues in Philosophy. St. Paul, MN: Paragon House, 2008. [An excellent two-volume collection of all key articles on global justice and global ethics.]

Rawls, John. *The Law of Peoples*. Cambridge: Harvard University Press, 1999. [A seminal book on how global community can be justly organized.]

Rothkopf, David. *Superclass*. New York: Farrar, Straus, and Giroux, 2008. [A new, and for the first time truly global, ruling class; who are they?]

Singer, Peter. *One World: The Ethics of Globalization*. New Haven: Yale University Press, 2002. [The strongest statement of cosmopolitan principles.]

Articles

Anand, Sudhir, and Paul Segal. "What Do We Know About Global Income Inequality?" *Journal of Economic Literature* 46, no. 1 (2008): 57–94. [Review of all the evidence up to the date of publication.]

Further Readings

Atkinson, Anthony B., and Andrea Brandolini. "Global World Inequality: Absolute, Relative, or Intermediate." Paper prepared for the twenty-eighth conference of the International Association for Research in Income and Wealth, Cork, Ireland, August 22–28, 2004. [Perhaps we should focus on increases in absolute inequality among individuals?]

Bourguignon, François, and Christian Morrisson. "The Size Distribution of Income Among World Citizens, 1820–1990." *American Economic Review* (September 2002): 727–744. [First empirical study of global inequality in its historical context.]

Milanovic, Branko. "Global Income Inequality: What It Is and Why It Matters." *World Economics* 7, no. 1 (2006): 131–153. [Empirics of global inequality and discussion of what, if anything, should be done about it.]

———. "True World Income Distribution, 1988 and 1993: First Calculation Based on Household Surveys Alone." *Economic Journal* 112, no. 476 (2002): 51–92. [A picture of the world conveyed by income surveys from about one hundred countries.]

Sutcliffe, Bob. "World Inequality and Globalization." *Oxford Review of Economic Policy* 20, no. 1 (2003): 15–37, 2003. [Review of the evidence and discussion of possible links between globalization and global inequality.]

Vignette 3.2

Friedman, Thomas. *The World Is Flat: A Brief History of the 21st Century.* New York: Farrar, Straus, and Giroux, 2006.

Milanovic, Branko, and Shlomo Yitzhaki. "Decomposing World Income Distribution: Does the World Have a Middle Class?" *Review of Income and Wealth* 48, no. 2 (2002): 155–178.

Pressman, Steven. "The Decline of the Middle Class: An International Perspective." *Journal of Economic Issues* 41, no. 1 (2007): 181–199.

Ravallion, Martin. *The Developing World's Bulging (but Vulnerable) "Middle Class."* Policy Research Working Paper no. 4816. Washington, DC: World Bank, January 2009.

Thurow, Lester. "A Surge of Inequality." *Scientific American* 256 (1987): 30–37.

Vignette 3.5

Milanovic, Branko "Globalization and Goals: Does Soccer Show the Way?" *Review of International Political Economy* 12, no. 5 (2005): 829–850.

Vignette 3.6

Atkinson, Tony. "Top Incomes in the United Kingdom over the Twentieth Century." Unpublished MS, December 2003.

Guriev, Sergei, and Andrei Rachinsky. "The Evolution of Personal Wealth in the Former Soviet Union and Central and Eastern Europe." In *Personal Wealth from a Global Perspective*, edited by James B. Davies. UNU-WIDER Studies in Development Economics. Oxford: Oxford University Press, 2008.

Piketty, Thomas, and Emmanuel Saez. "The Evolution of Top Incomes: A Historical and International Perspective." *American Economic Review* 96, no. 2 (2006): 200–205.

———. "Income Inequality in the United States, 1913–1998." *Quarterly Journal of Economics* 118, no. 1 (2003): 1–39.

Vignette 3.7

Milanovic, Branko, Peter H. Lindert, and Jeffrey G. Williamson. "Preindustrial Inequality." *Economic Journal*, forthcoming. Previous version published as *Measuring Ancient Inequality*. National Bureau of Economic Research Working Paper 13550. Cambridge, MA: National Bureau of Economic Research, 2009.

Vignette 3.8

Cohen, Joshua. "Comments on Rodrik." Unpublished MS.

Pogge, Thomas. "An Egalitarian Law of Peoples." *Philosophy and Public Affairs* 23, no. 3 (1994): 195–224.

Rawls, John. *The Law of Peoples*. Cambridge: Harvard University Press, 1999.

———. *A Theory of Justice*. Cambridge: Harvard University Press, 1971.

Risse, Mattias. "How Does Global Order Harm the Poor?" *Philosophy and Public Affairs* 33, no. 4 (2005): 349–376.

Singer, Peter. *One World: The Ethics of Globalization*. New Haven: Yale University Press, 2002.

Wenar, Leif. "Why Rawls Is Not a Cosmopolitan Egalitarian." In *Rawls' "Law of Peoples": A Realistic Utopia?* edited by R. Martin and D. Ready. Malden, MA: Blackwell, 2006.

Index

Abramovich, Roman, 40, 188
AC Milan soccer club, 187, 188, 191
Africa, 26, 51, 127, 168, 169, 209,
    214–215
    direct foreign investment in, 105
    economy in, 143
    Gini coefficient in, 31
    global inequality and, 157
    global middle class and, 173
    household surveys in, 150
    income divergence in, 101
    intercountry inequality and, 101, 110,
    130–134, 135–140
    migration and, 128–129
African Americans, 181
Agrarian reform, 54
Agriculture, 7, 46
Albania, 125, 126–127
Algeria, 52, 130, 133, 210
Amalrik, Andrei, 78
Andalusia, 51
Angola, 113
Anna Karenina (Tolstoy), 37–40
Anonymity principle, 24, 25
Arabs, 131
Argentina, 99, 184
Aristocracy, 88
Arkansas, 177
Armenia, 51
Aron, Raymond, 85–86
Arsenal, 188, 191
Asceticism, 13–14
Asia, 209

Gini coefficient in, 31
global inequality and, 157, 182–186
heterogeneity of, 182–183, 213–214
Latin America as mirror image of,
    182–186
Asia Minor, 51
Assimilation, 127–128
Atkinson, Anthony, 10, 19–20, 22
Aurelius, Marcus, 46–47
Austen, Jane, 33–36
Australia, 143, 144, 146, 168, 169
Austria, 52, 105

Balkans, 52
Banerjee, Abhijit, 10
Bangladesh, 127, 159, 182–183, 184
Bayern Munich soccer club, 187, 191
Beijing, China, 79, 80
Beitz, Charles, 162
Belgium, 52, 118
Bennet, Elizabeth, 33–35
Bennet, Mr., 33–35
Bennet, Mrs., 35, 39
Bensaad, Ali, 134
Bentham, Jeremy, 23
Berlusconi, Silvio, 132, 188
Between-component in inequality
    decomposition, 32
Bhagwati, Jagdish, 160
Big Bang analogy, 100
Bingley, Mr., 34
Bolivia, 168, 183, 184
Borussia Dortmund soccer club, 191

European Union (EU) (*continued*)
  interpersonal inequality and, 30, 77, 79
  soccer clubs and, 187–188
  United States vs., 176–181

Fanon, Frantz, 130
Fascism, 142
Feudalism, feudalists, 6
Finland, 177
Firebaugh, Glenn, 159
First World, 209–210, 211–212
Forbes magazine, 43, 44
Foreign investment, 5, 104
Fourth World, 212
France, 32, 51, 54, 75, 113, 146, 169
  direct foreign investment in, 105
  GDP per capita in, 144
  intercountry inequality and, 97, 99, 100, 118
  Parisian arrondissements in, 61–67
  price level in, 99
French Conseil National de la Recherche Scientifique, 64
Frontex, 131
Fujian, China, 80

Gansu, China, 80
Gates, Bill, 41, 43–44
Gaul, 51
GDP. *See* Gross domestic product
Geopolitics, 208–215
George III, King, 47
German Social Democrats, 111
Germany, 75, 118, 143, 146, 169
  intercountry inequality and, 109
  redistribution in, 70, 70fig
  soccer clubs in, 189–190
Ghana, 210
Gibbon, Edward, 47
Gilded Age, 194
Gillet, George, 188
Gini, Corrado, 25, 29

Gini coefficient, 29–31, 51, 53–54, 79, 90, 151–152, 176, 178
Global financial crisis, 193–197
Global inequality, 110, 112fig, 116fig
  Asia and, 182–186
  evolution of, 158–160
  GDP per capita in, 149
  geopolitics and, 208–215
  Gini coefficient and, 151–152
  global income distribution and, 165–170
  global middle class and, 171–175
  globalization and, 152, 154–156
  importance of, 160–163
  income divergence and, 153–154
  intercountry inequality and, 109–114, 115–119, 149, 150–151, 154
  interpersonal inequality and, 149
  justice and, 161–163
  Latin America and, 182–186
  measurement of, 149–150, 165–170, 198–202
  migration and, 204, 206
  poor and, 156–158
  Rawls, John and, 203–207
  soccer clubs and, 187–192
  tripartite classification and, 208–215
  ventile distributions and, 116–118
Global middle class, 103, 171–175
Globalization
  beneficiaries of, 141
  de-, 141–146
  global inequality and, 152, 154–156
  income divergence and, 104–108
  intercountry inequality and, 141–146
  Lucas paradox and, 106
  migration and, 204
  poor countries and, 104–107, 141–142
  soccer clubs and, 188
  technology and, 106–108, 141
  trilemma of, 163–164
Globalization 2.0, 104, 108, 142, 163, 212
  See also Globalization

Index